ANIME AND MANGA MEGA HANDBOOK

ISBN 978-1-339-01746-4

10 9 8 7 6 5 4 3 2 1   23 24 25 26 27

Printed in the U.S.A.   40
First printing 2023

ANIME AND MANGA MEGA HANDBOOK

SCHOLASTIC INC.

CONTENTS

TOP 10

BIG HITTERS

Who are the characters who punch above their weight with enough smarts and wit to take on all comers? Who are the greatest characters to leap out of the anime world? From martial-arts masters to element-wielding wonders and tiny-yet-titanic robots, here are our top 10 anime icons.

See page 12

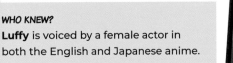

1 ONE PIECE
MONKEY D. LUFFY

CREATED BY Oda Eiichirō
MANGA 1997– **ANIME** 1999–

▶ Well, he had to top the list, didn't he? *One Piece* is the **number-one best-selling manga of all time** and much of that is due to this rubbery star. Thanks to him eating that Devil Fruit, not only is **Monkey D. Luffy** lively company, but he can stretch his fist to the size of a house and whack a foe at elastic speed. That's the **definition of a big hitter** right there!

WHO KNEW?
Luffy is voiced by a female actor in both the English and Japanese anime.

2 DRAGON BALL
SON GOKU

CREATED BY Toriyama Akira **MANGA** 1984–1995
ANIME 1986–1989, 1989–1996, 1996–1997, 2015–2018

▶ In his kid form or muscle-bound adult body, **Goku** is a prizefighter who deserves to be on this list. He has star quality and the ability to keep bouncing back with **five anime adaptations** and **21 animated movies** (plus a steady stream of video games). Even without his Super Saiyan form, **Goku** is one of the strongest mortals in the multiverse. As an infant he could pick up boulders and beat down a pteranodon—not many kids could make that claim! And did we mention how **350 million *Dragon Ball* books** have sold worldwide?

See page 60

WHO KNEW?
Goku is afraid of very little, except for needles.

3 BORUTO: NARUTO NEXT GENERATIONS
UZUMAKI BORUTO

CREATED BY Kishimoto Masashi
MANGA 2016– **ANIME** 2017–

▶ A chip off the old block, **Boruto** is as much of a champ as his dad, **Naruto**—he may just be a little more reckless and happy to take shortcuts! His **Uzumaki bloodline** has given him an advantage. He showed talent before enrolling at the Ninja Academy by creating Shadow Clones. **The Karma of Ōtsutsuki Momoshiki** gives him added power to tap into, but it threatens to take him over by rewriting his genetic pattern. This struggle to balance his powers with the risk of **Ōtsutsuki dominance** is something **Boruto** has to deal with. On the plus side, it gives him awesome temporary tattoos.

See page 38

WHO KNEW?
Boruto is the Japanese pronunciation of the English word **"bolt."**

See page 58

4 DR. SLUMP

NORIMAKI ARALE

CREATED BY Toriyama Akira **MANGA** 1980–1984 **ANIME** 1981–1986

▶ Now, hear us out. This cutie pie looks all innocent and **"wouldn't harm a fly,"** but she's also one of the strongest characters in anime. Invented by the quirky and rather useless Professor Norimaki Senbē, **Arale** is a robot with poor eyesight and a naive personality. But she does have the superstrength to move planets around! She can also headbutt foes, sending them soaring hundreds of miles up. She's fought *Dragon Ball*'s **Goma** to a draw and that's with just a fraction of her power. Never underestimate the little guys!

WHO KNEW?
Arale's name is a play on the Japanese word for rice cracker, *"arare."*

See page 98

5 BLEACH

KUROSAKI ICHIGO

CREATED BY Kubo Noriaki **MANGA** 2001–2016 **ANIME** 2004–2012

▶ After taking on the role of a **Shinigami**, or **Soul Reaper**, **Ichigo** is a determined defender against evil Hollows and sends them on their merry way to the **Soul Society** (in pieces if necessary!). He has a strong sense of honor and will always protect his friends, but you wouldn't want to get on the wrong side of him. **Ichigo** performs all his **Soul Reaper duties** without skipping his schoolwork. Plus, he has great hair . . . don't let anyone say otherwise.

WHO KNEW?
15 is a significant number for **Ichigo**. It's his birthday, the age he became a substitute Shinigami, and his bedroom door number. **15** is also a pun on his name with **"Ichi"** meaning **1** and **"go"** meaning **5** in Japanese.

See page 54

6   DEMON SLAYER
##

CREATED BY Gotōge Koyoharu **MANGA** 2016–2020 **ANIME** 2019–

▶ Her brother **Tanjirō** gets a lot of credit for taking revenge on hordes of demons and trying to remove his sibling's curse, but his sister is often strongest in battle. Having received a huge dose of blood from the **demon king Muzan**, **Kamado Nezuko** has managed to restrain her desire to attack humans. As well as this inner strength, she has plenty of demon powers to take to the fight—especially in her **full berserk demon form**. She has skills that even the **Twelve Kizuki** can't conquer, such as her ability to regain her strength without sipping human blood and being in the sun without dying!

WHO KNEW?
As demons don't age, **Nezuko** remains the age she was when attacked, which is 12.

7   ASTRO BOY
ASTRO BOY

See page 112

CREATED BY Tezuka Osamu **MANGA** 1952–1968 **ANIME** 1963, 1980, 2003

▶ The boy robot deserves his place in the top 10—not just because he's got the strength of an army, but because the character is such an inspiration for generations of creators. You could say his creator, **Tezuka Osamu**, and *Astro Boy* are the foundation of all that followed in manga and anime. Known as **Tetsuwan Atom (Mighty Atom)** in Japan, **Astro Boy** tries to avoid conflict. But when necessary, he can take off with his foot jets and 100,000 horsepower engine and fire lasers from his arm. Don't let this robot kid turn his back on you—he has a pair of cannons that can slide out from his behind!

WHO KNEW?
Astro Boy was featured in a series of Japanese road-safety videos.

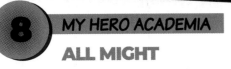

8 MY HERO ACADEMIA
ALL MIGHT

CREATED BY Horikoshi Kōhei
MANGA 2014– **ANIME** 2016–

▶ **"I am here!" All Might** was Japan's **number-one superhero** and is an idol to nerdy **Midoriya Izuku**. He's superstrong, superfast, and tough, but he hides serious injuries from a battle with **All For One**. While **Izuku** may be due a place in these rankings for his fast progress through the Hero Program, **All Might** is his mentor and inspiration. And by managing to be a selfless hero while fragile in his true state, he deserves our respect.

See page 26

WHO KNEW?
All Might's signature moves are named after US states. His ultimate move is the **United States of Smash**.

9 FULLMETAL ALCHEMIST
EDWARD ELRIC

CREATED BY Arakawa Hiromu
MANGA 2001–2010 **ANIME** 2003–2004, 2009–2010

▶ If clawing one's way back from disaster accounts for anything, **Edward Elric** deserves the number-one spot. After losing an arm and leg (and his brother) when a Human Transmutation attempt went wrong, Edward persevered and became the **youngest-ever State Alchemist**. He then set off to claim the **Philosopher's Stone**—hoping it might restore his brother's body while his soul is housed in a suit of armor. He has undergone serious martial-arts training, boosted by his prosthetic arm and leg, which give him extra offensive capabilities. Regardless of his fighting prowess, we're putting him on the list purely for his **dedication to bringing back his brother**.

See page 146

WHO KNEW?
Edward has claimed to be 165 cm (5 ft 5 in) tall, but that includes his **raised shoes** and **spiky hair**. He's really 141 cm (4 ft 8 in).

See page 94

SAILOR MOON
SAILOR MOON

CREATED BY Takeuchi Naoko **MANGA** 1991–1997 **ANIME** 1992–1997, 2014–

▶ **"In the name of the Moon, I'll punish you!"** One of the first anime characters to really hit it big on the international stage was *Sailor Moon*—a doe-eyed power princess. **Tsukino Usagi** can look all cutesy and is a real sucker for kittens (who isn't?!), but, once she takes on her magical form, she can beat the best of them. She has power endowed to her through a magical brooch but is especially great when teamed up with the rest of the **Sailor Guardians**. With a **Moon Frisbee** (tiara), **Spiral Heart Moon Rod**, **Moon Gorgeous Meditation**, and **Starlight Honeymoon Therapy Kiss**, she has the best-named attacks at her disposal. Plus, how many heroes can fire projectiles from their hairpins?!

ONE PIECE
(Wan Pīsu)

What more can you say about *One Piece*? It's officially the best-selling manga title ever, with over 517 million copies in circulation in 61 countries. Acclaimed for its characters, world-building, and humor-packed battles, the record-breaking manga series by Oda Eiichirō is a worldwide phenomenon. To satisfy the huge demand, three million copies of each tankōbon are printed. Over a thousand anime episodes and 15 movies have followed in the wake of the Going Merry. These pirates have struck gold!

BREAKDOWN

▶ *One Piece* is set in a world with two great oceans divided by a mountainous range called the **Red Line** and ruled by a **corrupt World Government**. Inspired by his idol, the pirate **Red-Haired Shanks**, teenager **Monkey D. Luffy** sets out to form his own pirate crew and locate the "One Piece"—the legendary lost treasure of Gold Roger. Having eaten the **Gum-Gum Devil Fruit** (one of the secret treasures of the sea), **Luffy's** entire body can stretch like rubber. Ironically, his elastic powers mean he sinks if he falls in the sea.

SNAPSHOT

▶ Writer/artist **Oda Eiichirō** launched his manga career in 1992, at age 17. He created a one-shot cowboy story *Wanted!* before gaining experience as an assistant for a number of major manga artists. **Oda** was inspired to write a story about pirates after watching the cartoon series *Vicky the Viking* as a child. Drawing from real-life biographies of pirates, and inspired by **Toriyama Akira's** manga *Dragon Ball*, Oda developed his tale of **Monkey D. Luffy.** He planned to wrap it up in five years, but he enjoyed the work so much, he just kept on going. And here we are over 20 years later!

THE CORE

MANGA

PUBLISHED BY: Shueisha
36 volumes, 2014–
WRITER/ARTIST: Oda Eiichirō
SPIN-OFFS: *Cross Epoch* (One Piece/Dragon Ball crossover) 2006
Taste of the Devil Fruit 2011
One Piece Party 2015–

ANIME

PRODUCED FOR: Toei Animation 1999–
WRITERS: Takegami Junki, Kamisaka Hirohiko, Yonemura Shōji
1,045 episodes
13 TV specials
7 OVAs (ORIGINAL VIDEO ANIMATIONS)

MOVIES

One Piece: The Movie 2000
Clockwork Island Adventure 2001
Chopper's Kingdom on the Island of Strange Animals 2002
Dead End Adventure 2003
The Cursed Holy Sword 2004
Baron Omatsuri and the Secret Island 2005
Giant Mecha Soldier of Karakuri Castle 2006
The Desert Princess and the Pirates: Adventures in Alabasta 2007
Episode of Chopper Plus: Bloom in the Winter Miracle Cherry Blossom 2008
One Piece Film: Strong World 2009
Straw Hat Chase 2011
One Piece Film: Z 2012
One Piece Film: Gold 2016
One Piece: Stampede 2019
One Piece Film: Red 2022

GRINDING GEARS

Luffy gained his stretchy power by eating a **Gum-Gum Devil Fruit**. More than just a human elastic band, Luffy has learned to boost his power with several gear changes.

▶ GEAR 2

By increasing his blood flow, **Luffy** can enlarge his muscles, move his limbs like whips, and surround his fists with flames he calls **Red Hawk**.

▶ GEAR 3

By blowing air into his thumb, **Luffy** can enlarge specific parts of his body and give them colossal strength—enough to topple buildings!

▶ GEAR 4

By blowing into his arm, **Luffy** can pump up his muscles to mega-size and coat them with an invisible armor, **Busoshoku Haki**.

▶ GEAR 5

Making the most of his **Devil Fruit**, **Luffy** can take on the form of the **Sun God Nika**, allowing him to grow cartoonishly giant, and turn other people and objects rubbery.

UNBEATABLE

▶ *One Piece Film: Red* was the number-one box-office hit in Japan in 2022, earning **18.78 billion yen** (US $141.6 million) over a six-month run in theaters. The movie is currently the **sixth biggest-grossing anime movie** in the country and ninth in any movie category.

THE VOID CENTURY

▶ The final arc for the manga *One Piece* is near, but where will that take the **Straw Hat Pirates**? One major mystery begging to be resolved is that of the **Void Century**—a 100-year gap in history that led to the establishment of the World Government. The government bans research into it. If the **Straw Hats** are to find out the truth about their world, they need this information.

▶ When the government found out that the archaeologists of Ohara were attempting to decipher poneglyphs (stone slabs inscribed with a mysterious ancient script) that described the missing period, they ordered the island's destruction. The attack on undefended archaeologists convinced the giant marine **vice admiral Jaguar D. Saul** to switch allegiances. He saved the young **Nico Robin** but was apparently killed during the assault on the island.

▶ This proved not to be so. Saul survived and led a team of giants to recover the archaeologists' research. The work is now in safekeeping with the giants on the **island of Elbaf**. A visit now seems certain for **Luffy's** crew, with archaeologist **Nico Robin** one of only two living people able to read the poneglyph scripts. Revelations about the **Void Century** are sure to shake things up.

▶ Will **Luffy** finally get his hands on the elusive One Piece treasure? Its discovery is said to signal **"a grand battle that will engulf the entire world,"** according to the pirate Whiteboard . . . Uh-oh!

THE STRAW HAT PIRATES

▶ **Luffy** has recruited a diverse crew over the years by impressing them with his talent and blind optimism. Early crew members aboard the good ship *Going Merry* include the swordsman **Roronoa "Pirate Hunter" Zero**, thief and navigator **Nami**, sniper **Usopp**, cook **Sanji**, talking reindeer doctor **Tony Tony Chopper**, archaeologist **Nico Robin**, cola-powered cyborg shipwright **Franky**, and **Brook** the musical skeleton.

MAKING AN ENTRANCE

▶ At the 2021 Tokyo Olympics, long-jump gold medalist **Miltiádis Tentóglou** of Greece shared his love for *One Piece*. He replicated **Monkey D. Luffy's** signature **Gear Second pose** during his broadcast entrance.

WHERE NEXT?

If you love *One Piece*, try:

▶ **NARUTO** (PICTURED)
Uzumaki Naruto heads on a quest to control the demonic fox within him, to become an adept ninja and leader of his village.

▶ **DRAGON BALL**
Oda Eiichirō has admitted being hugely influenced by the original *Dragon Ball* series. It's a tale of a young protagonist, **Son Goku**, seeking seven powerful **Dragon Balls**.

▶ **HUNTER x HUNTER**
A young boy, **Gon**, leaves home to train as a Hunter just like his missing father. He passes difficult tests and makes many friends along the way.

SPY X FAMILY

(Supai Famirī)

A fairly new addition to manga's hall of fame, *Spy x Family* (you don't need to pronounce the "x") is an action comedy about a spy's attempts to go undercover as a family man. While the plot involves Cold War espionage, there's a sweet family dynamic at the heart of the series. Agent Twilight, his recruited wife, and his adopted daughter try to play the role of a happy family while hiding their own secrets.

BREAKDOWN

▶ To maintain a truce between the rival states of Westalis and Ostania, **Westalian intelligence agent and master of disguise "Twilight"** is ordered to spy on **Donovan Desmond**, the leader of the **National Unity Party** within Ostania. To get close to Desmond, **Twilight** poses as a psychiatrist, **Loid Forger**, and adopts a child to enroll in the same elite private school as **Desmond**. Unbeknownst to **Twilight**, his new daughter, **Anya**, is a **mind-reader** and **Yor Briar**, the wife he recruits, is secretly the **top assassin** known as **Thorn Princess**. To make matters even more tangled, the pretend family also adopt a dog called **Bond**, which has an ability to **see into the future**.

SNAPSHOT

▶ By the time **Endō Tatsuya** launched *Spy x Family*, he had been working with his editor **Lin Shihei** for a decade on the manga series *Tista* (2007), featuring a **young female assassin,** and *Gekka Bijin* (2010), about an exiled moon princess on Earth. Lin encouraged Endō to develop a manga aimed at a **younger audience** than his early work. *Spy x Family* ticks that box with its mix of action and cute comedy. Within two years of its debut, *Spy x Family* was picked up to be adapted for an anime series.

THE CORE
MANGA
PUBLISHED BY: Shueisha
10 volumes, 2019–
WRITER/ARTIST: Endō Tatsuya
ANIME
PRODUCED FOR: Wit Studios 2022–
WRITER: Furuhashi Kazuhiro
25 episodes

OPERATION STRIX

▶ **Operation Strix** is **Twilight's** mission to get close to the leader of the National Unity Party, **Donovan Desmond**. They must stop him from shattering the fragile peace between Westalis and Ostania. **Desmond** is rarely seen in public, so **Twilight** has to infiltrate his private life. For **Twilight**, this means adopting the identity of the psychiatrist **Loid Forger**. He's a husband and father of a student at **Eden Academy**, where **Desmond's son Damian** goes. Getting close to **Desmond** requires Loid's "daughter" **Anya** to make a success of her studies. Unfortunately, she has little academic ability (though she can read the minds of those who know exam answers!), so it takes a while for her to befriend **Damian**. But **Damian** is slowly developing a crush on **Anya**.

SINGING SPIES

▶ How about *Spy x Family* the Musical? Yes, an adaptation is underway to bring the manga to life onstage with songs. *Musical Spy × Family* debuted at Tokyo's Imperial Theater in **March 2023** before going on tour. The show has hired **four girls to share the role of Anya**. The screenplay and lyrics are by the composer **Kamimura Shuhei**.

COLD WAR

▶ **Westalis** and **Ostania** are versions of the **real-life West and East Germany**—a country divided by the **Berlin Wall** during the second half of the 20th Century. **Berlint = Berlin.** Ostania boasts an equivalent of East Germany's secret police, the Stasi, in the SSS. It even has a version of the **Trabant,** which was a famously poorly made car driven behind the Berlin Wall. The division of Germany followed **World War II,** and there are hints in *Spy x Family* of **Twilight's** troubled childhood in the midst of war.

BECAUSE IT REMINDS ME OF MY CHILDHOOD.

UNDERCOVER

▶ *Spy x Family* includes several not-very-subtle references to other classic spy series. **Anya's** former codename is **"Test Subject 007."** The Forgers' bow-tie-wearing dog is named **Bond**—after **Anya's** favorite character, **Bondman** (in the comic and TV show *Spy Wars*). Plus, the way **Twilight** receives orders, along with his skill with disguises, is very *Mission: Impossible.*

FROSTY FEMME

▶ **Yor** has a rival for **Loid's** affection, and her name is **Fiona Frost**. A fellow Westalian intelligence agent, **Frost** goes under the codename **"Nightfall"** and acts as **Twilight's** assistant in an undercover role at the Berlint General Hospital. While cold on the outside, **Frost** harbors a secret love for **Loid** and wishes to replace **Yor** as his partner. Her desires risk undermining Operation Strix.

SECOND WIND

▶ A **second season** for the anime, along with a full animated movie for *Spy x Family*, were announced at Jump Festa '23. Both are expected to premiere in 2023. **Endō Tatsuya** is writing an original story for the movie, as well as supervising the production and providing original character designs.

▶ In *Spy x Family* Season 2, you can expect to see the relationship between **Anya** and **Damian Desmond** develop as Operation Strix continues following **Loid** and **Desmond's** first meeting. Plus, in an adaptation of the "Great Cruise Adventure," the Forgers head out on their first family vacation, providing a new challenge for **Yor**.

WHERE NEXT?

If you love *Spy x Family*, try:

▶ **KOTARO LIVES ALONE**
Kotaro is a four-year-old boy who (as the title says) lives without parental guidance. But he is soon adopted by his neighbors and one of them is a struggling manga author.

▶ **SWEETNESS AND LIGHTNING**
While this slice-of-life anime lacks the action and espionage of *Spy x Family*, it shares the focus on family relationships. There's a teacher trying to raise his young daughter as a single parent through cooking.

▶ **FULL METAL PANIC! FUMOFFU** (PICTURED)
This *Full Metal Panic!* spin-off and slapstick delight sees **Sagara Sōsuke** go undercover at school to protect **Chidori Kaname** from mecha threats.

TOP 10

SPORTS ANIME

Sports is a massive genre in manga and anime. Fans track the efforts of school friends hoping to make the team, or professionals gaining superstar status. The range of sports is epic, from basketball to skateboarding, archery to figure skating, and even tankery! With charming characters, bitter rivalries, teamwork trials, and edge-of-your-seat competitions, here are 10 that deserve a place among the all-stars.

1 HAIKYŪ!!
VOLLEYBALL

▶ You have to be tall to make it big in **volleyball**, right? Well, being short in stature doesn't stop **Hinata Shōyō** from aiming high. *Haikyū!!* is a **long-running volleyball classic**. It follows **Shōyō** from junior high school as he sets up a school club, tackles his first tournament, deals with defeats and competitors, and eventually takes aim at the Nationals.

▶ The story has **well-developed central characters** led by **Shōyō** and his rival-turned-teammate **Kageyama Tobio**, as they build up the skill and team spirit to succeed. With gripping **slo-mo on-court action**, *Haikyū!!* puts you right in the game.

2 · SK∞ THE INFINITY
SKATEBOARDING

▶ Sophomore Okinawa high school skateboarder **Kyan Reki** is obsessed with taking his sport to the limits. He joins fellow skaters racing along a **secret, no-holds-barred course in an abandoned mine. "Beefs"** run riot as skaters are allowed to attack opponents. This is the dangerous world of "S."

▶ After an injury, **Reki** invites Canadian snowboarder/skating newbie, **Hasegawa Ranga**, to join him in the race. "S" also tempts a range of outrageous characters to tackle the course. They include a cackling punk-clown named **Shadow** (think Batman's Joker), a superintelligent AI skater named **Cherry Blossom**, a buffed-up speedster named **Joe**, and the masked "Matador of Love," **Adam**. It's supercharged fun with dynamic direction from **Utsumi Hiroko** and convincing skate moves based on pros like **Rodney Mullen**.

3 · TSURUNE
ARCHERY

▶ What if you mixed the bow and arrow with martial arts? That's what you get with **kyūdō**—a form of archery that originated with the **samurai** during **feudal-era Japan**. Having quit **kyūdō** at middle school after suffering target panic (letting loose his arrow too early), teenager **Narumiya Minato** returns to the sport at high school after meeting a mysterious man on a forest archery range. **Minato** joins the **Kazemai High School Kyūdō Club** and progresses with his team toward the Nationals.

▶ This is not high-octane anime, but it makes for calm and reflective viewing. And, if you're wondering, **"tsurune"** is the twanging sound of a bowstring after the arrow is released.

4 BLUE LOCK
SOCCER

▶ Japan's **national soccer squad** has been leaping up the rankings year on year as their 2022 appearance in the **World Cup knockout-stage** proved. Had they followed the *Blue Lock* method, who knows how much further they would have risen! *Blue Lock* is set in the wake of the 2018 competition, with the Japanese Football Union hiring a new coach—the mysterious **Ego Jinpachi**. Ego sets up a **soccer boot camp** named *Blue Lock* to produce the world's greatest striker. Plucked from high school is young prodigy **Isagi Yoichi**—it's his progress among 300 candidates that we follow. As the name suggests, **Ego Jinpachi** is seeking a striker with major self-assurance. This is less a story about teamwork and more about achieving the drive to succeed above others.

5 ACE OF DIAMOND
BASEBALL

▶ **Baseball** is the **number-one sport in Japan**, so it's no surprise to see it covered in depth in manga and anime. *Ace of Diamond* stars a young pitcher, **Sawamura Eijun**, who has a unique style that sends the baseball on **unpredictable trajectories**. The school sports star is soon spotted by a scout and enrolled at the elite **Seido High School**. Here he is joined by gifted catcher **Kazuya Miyuki** in a team aiming to reach the **Koushien championships**.

▶ Reaching the top requires plenty of grit and hard work for the team. Even if you're not a fan of the sport, *Ace of Diamond* will soon have you rooting for the heroes.

6 KUROKO'S BASKETBALL
BASKETBALL

▶ The **Teikō Middle School basketball team** won the middle school Nationals for three years in a row, thanks to star players known as the **"Generation of Miracles."** The five went their separate ways, graduating to new schools and new basketball teams. *Kuroko's Basketball* follows the path of a sixth forgotten member of this genius generation, **Kuroko Tetsuya**. Along with another talent, **Kagami Taiga**, **Kuroko** sets his sights on taking his new school team at Seirin High to the top, by defeating the rest of the famed **Generation of Miracles**. While the on-court action is not as realistic as *Slam Dunk*, *Kuroko's Basketball* has a lot of appeal with its focus on special moves and the interactions between different characters.

7 YURI ON ICE
FIGURE SKATING

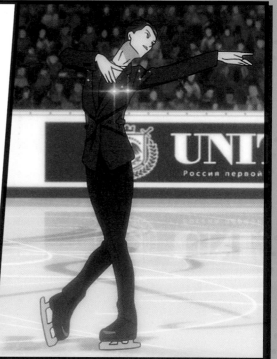

▶ A story of competition, expression, and romance, *Yuri on Ice stands* out among the more formulaic sports anime output. After a series of losses, Japanese figure skater **Katsuki Yūri** puts his international career on hold and returns home to **Kyushu**. After one of his skating routines is shared online, **Yūri** attracts the attention of the Russian figure-skating champion **Victor Nikiforov**, who offers to be his coach. To confuse matters, **Victor** has promised to work with another **Yuri**, **Yuri Plisetsky**, who is a Russian prodigy. When Victor chooses **Katsuki**, the stage is set for both Yuris to compete against each other in the **Grand Prix Final**. As the competition continues, the relationship between **Victor** and **Yūri** becomes more than just coach and mentee.

8 GIRLS UND PANZER
TANK WARFARE

▶ Yes, you read that correctly. *Girls und Panzer* features a sports competition between girls' high schools using tanks! Adding **military mischief** to the sports genre, the series has **World War II–era tanks** included as a **martial-arts class option**, **Sensha-dō**, or **tankery**. The main protagonist is **Nishizumi Miho**, who (after a tank-driving trauma at her previous school) is reluctant to be involved with Sensha-dō again. But just after she enrolls at the **Ōarai Girls' Academy** (aboard an aircraft carrier!), the school starts Sensha-dō classes and insists that she joins them. If the school fails to win the National Championships, it will be forced to close.

▶ With a premise like this, it's obvious *Girls und Panzer* is staged for laughs. With varied personalities and well-staged tank battles, the show has become a huge hit. Model tanks from the show are selling out in Japan, and there are **11 different manga series** being published.

9 HAJIME NO IPPO
BOXING

▶ *Hajime no Ippo* literally translates as **The First Step**. Well, it's certainly been a long stride for this classic sports manga and anime—**34 years** and still fighting in its corner! The adventure follows shy high school student **Makunouchi Ippo**, who, after being saved from a serious beating by bullies, is taken to a gym where he takes out his frustrations and shows natural fighting ability. Through many trials, knock-backs, and a tough training regime, **Makunouchi** slowly punches his way toward becoming a champion.

▶ *Hajime no Ippo* wins not just because of its hard-hitting matches but also through the insights it provides into each fighter's motivations.

10 THE PRINCE OF TENNIS
TENNIS

▶ Unusually for a sports anime, *The Prince of Tennis* has a lead character who is already good at his game. **Echizen Ryōma** is a tennis prodigy who attends **Seishun Academy Tokyo** and soon discovers he can outplay his seniors. He is then on the way toward entering the **National Middle School Tennis Championship**, making new friends, and developing his technique. As he becomes a better player, **Ryōma** discovers just how important the sport is to him. This series can be somewhat repetitive, but it features a good range of characters to keep you watching set after set.

MY HERO ACADEMIA
(Boku no Hīrō Akademia)

One of the best-selling manga titles in history, *My Hero Academia* has over 65 million copies in circulation. It's a huge hit, with six seasons of the regular show (so far), heaps of movies, and numerous spin-offs such as light novels, stage plays, trading cards, and video games. The big draws are its inventive character designs and explosive battles. There is also a convincing evolution for its likable lead, Midoriya Izuku.

BREAKDOWN

▶ *My Hero Academia* is set in a world where **80 percent of the world's population** are superhuman with powers called **"Quirks."** The 14-year-old hero fanboy **Izuku** dreams of enrolling in the **Hero Program** at U.A. High School but never developed a **Quirk** in his childhood. But **Izuku** proves he has the courage to be a hero by taking on a supervillain to save his classmate **Bakugō Katsuki**. Then **All Might** (his idol and **Japan's number-one superhero**) gives **Izuku** his own **One for All Quirk** so he can fulfill his ambition and train to be a champion.

THE FIRST HERO

▶ **Horikoshi** revisited a one-shot titled *My Hero (Boku no Hīrō)* (PICTURED) when developing his long-term plan for *My Hero Academia*. Published in the 2008 Winter Issue of Japanese title *Akamaru Jump*, *My Hero* features an unpowered salaryman named **Jack Midoriya** who helps sell gadgets for heroes while dreaming of becoming a hero himself. As a trial run, it's quite basic, and **Jack** is nowhere as engaging as the younger **Izuku**. But his courage against an overpowering foe, and the respect he gains from the hero Positive, mirrors the origin of **Izzy** and **All Might**.

TO ME, YOU'RE MY HERO.

THE CORE

MANGA
PUBLISHED BY: Shueisha
36 volumes, 2014–
WRITER/ARTIST: Horikoshi Kōhei
SPIN-OFFS: *Smash!!* 2015–2017
Vigilantes 2016–2022
Team-Up Missions 2019–

ANIME
PRODUCED FOR: Bones Studio 2016–
WRITER: Kuroda Yōsuke
122 episodes
8 OVAs (ORIGINAL VIDEO ANIMATIONS)

MOVIES
Two Heroes 2018
Heroes Rising 2019
World Heroes' Mission 2021

RECORD-BREAKING

My Hero Academia holds the record for the most nominations and wins at the annual **Crunchyroll anime awards**. It has received **27 nominations** and **15 awards** over the six years of the global event.

SEASON SIX

▶ The 2022–2023 season of the anime *My Hero Academia* follows the huge battle between U.A. High School students and the **villainous Paranormal Liberation Front**, the **merged League of Villains**, and **Meta Liberation Army**. It's led by **Shigaraki Tomura**, the **Symbol of Evil**. The 25-episode season covers this **"Paranormal Liberation War"** that was featured in the manga's 18th story arc (volumes 26–31).

Following intel from **Pro Hero Hawks**, the heroes have the information they need to confront the merged villain group in an all-out war. This will deliver major consequences for hero society and the citizens they are entrusted to protect, plus the untimely fall of one fan favorite.

ALLIES/RIVALS

▶ At the core of *My Hero Academia* is **Midoriya** and **Bakugō's** relationship. Friends from childhood, the pair became rivals at school as **Katsuki's Quirk** manifested while **Izuku's** failed to materialize. **Katsuki** bullied **Izuku** to deter him from following his path to U.A. High School and bore a grudge even when the powerless **Izuku** tried to save him from the **Sludge Villain**. Once the duo enrolled in the **Hero Program**, and **Izuku** had a **Quirk** to utilize, **Katsuki** felt jealous of his classmate's progress and actively engaged him in battle. On the eve of the **Paranormal Liberation War**, however, the pair are more willing to work as allies.

ONE FOR ALL

▶ Midoriya Izuku—hero name **Deku**—is the ninth host for the **One For All Quirk** transferred to him from **All Might**. It allows **Izuku** to access the Quirks of its previous wielders and communicate with them. The **One For All Quirk** cannot be stolen—it is donated willingly by its owner. As such, it is an effective Quirk to use against **All For One**, who has the power to steal superpowers.

The Quirks wielded so far by **Deku** include:

Transmission—the power to change the speed of its possessor or anything he touches.

Fa Jin—the storing and release of kinetic energy as explosive bursts of power and speed.

Danger Sense—local threat detection.

Blackwhip—the power to direct black-energy streams to capture objects and foes.

Smokescreen—the power to create dense clouds of smoke.

Float—levitation.

LIVE ACTION

▶ **Legendary Entertainment**—home of the blockbuster *Enola Holmes, Pokémon Detective Pikachu* (PICTURED), and *Dune* movies—have a live-action adaptation of *My Hero Academia* in the works. *Kingdom* director Shinsuke Sato is set to make his English-language debut with the feature.

THE FINAL ACT

▶ **Horikoshi Kōhei** has suggested the manga *My Hero Academia* is close to its climax—2023 is a possible date for a wrap-up that has been planned from the outset. When volume 34 came out, **Horikoshi** expressed bittersweet feelings over concluding **Izuku** and **Katsuki's** adventures. Volume 36 is already out in Japan, while English volumes 33 and 34 are due in 2023.

WHERE NEXT?

If you love *My Hero Academia*, try:

▶ **FIRE FORCE** (PICTURED)
A **Special Fire Force** graduate joins a pyrokinetic firefighting team to take on supernatural "infernals."

▶ **LITTLE WITCH ACADEMIA**
Teenage **Akko** joins a school for witches, though she has no magical powers of her own. Sound familiar?

▶ **BORUTO: NARUTO NEXT GENERATIONS**
Horikoshi cites **Naruto** as an inspiration. That's a good enough reason to seek out this ninja tale.

GOLDEN KAMUY
(Gōruden Kamui)

Historic seinen manga *Golden Kamuy* is a dramatic and thoughtful journey through a Japan wracked by war. There is a quest for hidden gold, issues of indigenous rights, and fictionalized real-life characters and events. The manga has some violence (less so in the anime), but it's the relationship between Sugimoto and Asirpa that is the core of the story. The scarred war veteran tries to protect the Ainu girl from the brutal reality of conflict as she tries to keep him to his promise of no killing.

BREAKDOWN

▶ In Meiji-period **Hokkaido** (following the **Russo-Japanese War**), war-veteran-turned-gold-panner, **Sugimoto "Immortal" Saichi** is approached by an old man who tells him a tale of lost gold. The gold can only be found by joining **24 maps** tattooed onto a group of escaped prisoners. **Sugimoto** doubts the story, but after the old man is killed by a bear, such a tattoo is revealed on his body. **Sugimoto** is saved from the bear by a young indigenous girl, **Asirpa**. She joins him on the hunt for the gold, and the pair gain allies during their quest to complete the map. They also have to deal with a dangerous assortment of criminals and a ruthless army division.

SNAPSHOT

▶ **Noda Satoru** named the lead character in his historical epic after his own great-grandfather, who was a veteran of the Russo-Japanese War. **Noda** was born on the island of **Hokkaido** (where the saga is set) before relocating to Tokyo to begin his manga apprenticeship under **Kunitomo Yasuyuki**, the creator of manga *10 Billion Men (100-oku no Otoko)*. After a decade as an assistant, **Noda** got his break with the serialized sports manga *Supinamarada!* in 2011.

▶ In 2014, **Noda** launched *Golden Kamuy*. This won the **Manga Taishō award** in 2016 and the **Tezuka Osamu Cultural Prize** in 2018—the same year the manga was adapted for anime. He finally completed *Golden Kamuy* in 2022 and announced his return to the world of *Supinamarada!*

THE CORE
MANGA
PUBLISHED BY: Shueisha
31 volumes, 2014–2022
WRITER/ARTIST: Noda Satoru
ANIME
PRODUCED FOR: Geno Studio,
Brain's Base 2018–
WRITER: Takagi Noboru
42 episodes
3 OVAs

ASIRPA AND THE AINU

▶ **Asirpa** is a young, very capable member of the indigenous group the **Ainu**. This group faced injustice during the Meiji period of Japanese history. *Golden Kamuy* shares much about their culture and connection to nature, where animals are seen as **god-like**, or **kamuy**. **Asirpa** is not interested in the gold that **Sugimoto** seeks but in protecting her people's culture and history. On her journey with **Sugimoto**, she discovers secrets about her father and her connection to the tattooed maps. Will she fulfill her father's dream and lead the **Ainu** to independence?

▶ The **Ainu** are a real-life indigenous group that lived in **Hokkaido** and **islands off the coast of Russia**. The population saw their lands handed over to Japanese farmers in the late 19th century and the suppression of their culture. Many **Ainu** became part of Japanese society but their culture has been kept alive by a few hundred native **Ainu** speakers. The **Ainu** people were finally acknowledged as an indigenous people with rights in 1997.

FACT OR FICTION?

▶ Although **Noda Satoru** said he is more focused on telling an interesting story than **historical accuracy**, a lot of *Golden Kamuy* is based on fact. The manga highlights lots of **native wildlife** and elements of **Ainu culture** as captions alongside the story. **Noda** spent a year researching **Ainu culture** for the series, with help from **Nakagawa Hiroshi**, a professor of **Ainu language** at Chiba University. The assassination of **Tsar Alexander II of Russia** in 1881 is one historical event featured that did actually take place—though **Noda** has altered it to involve the characters **Will** and **Kiroranke**.

OPPOSING FORCES

▶ The **Russo-Japanese War** was fought between the Russian Empire and Empire of Japan beginning in 1904. It was over territorial claims to parts of Korea and Manchuria (China). The war took place over land and sea with the Japanese winning many major victories, but at the cost of tens of thousands of lives. Peace was finally brokered by **US President Theodore Roosevelt** in 1905.

LIVE FROM THE FRONT

As announced in spring 2022, a live-action treatment of *Golden Kamuy* is in the works for movie release.

THE 7TH DIVISION

▶ **Sugimoto** and **Asirpa** are not alone in seeking the hidden gold. The **7th Division** led by **Tsurumi Tokushirō** had been on the case before **Sugimoto** was made aware of the loot. The **7th Division** were seen as the strongest unit in the Japanese army and sent into the worst fighting during the war's **siege of Port Arthur** and **Battle of Mukden**. While **Sugimoto** has a selfless plan for the gold (helping the widow of one of his fallen comrades), **Tsurumi** wants to use it to fund a military coup that will create an independent **Hokkaido**.

WHERE NEXT?

If you love *Golden Kamuy*, try:

▶ HOUSE OF FIVE LEAVES

For more **historical drama**, *House of Five Leaves* is set during the **Edo Period**. This anime follows a timid ronin, **Masanosuke Akitsu**, who becomes the bodyguard for the leader of a group of bandits named the **Five Leaves**.

▶ HAKUOUKI (PICTURED)

In feudal Japan of 1894, a young woman named **Yukimura Chizuru** goes in search of her missing father. After witnessing a brutal attack, she is rescued by the **Shinsengumi**, a military rōnin unit who share her mission.

▶ RUROUNI KENSHIN

Set during the same period as *Golden Kamuy*, *Rurouni Kenshin* is the story of a **nomadic swordsman** who quit killing but can't escape from his violent past.

HOW TO DRAW...

EXPRESSIONS

Express yourself and the emotions of your manga characters with this step-by-step guide to drawing faces.

STEP 1

For a male, draw an oval shape for the head, pinched to a point for the chin. Add large eyes and ears just below the halfway mark, plus eyebrows above.

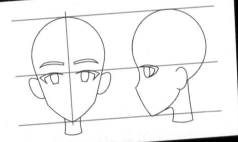

STEP 2

A simple notch works for the nose. The mouth sits halfway between the nose and chin.

STEP 3

Sketch a mop of unruly hair with curls sweeping from the crown. Shade in the eyelashes and pupils in the eyes.

STEP 1

A female head has the same shape as the male, but the eyes are larger and sit right in the middle.

STEP 2

A short, vertical line is all you need for the nose, with a smile added below.

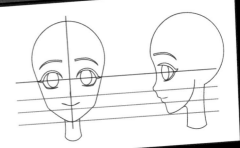

STEP 3

The girl's hair is parted on the left, with bangs sweeping down. Her dark pupils feature a white circle, top right, where light is reflected.

SURPRISE

For a surprised expression, draw high eyebrows, wide-open eyes, and a tiny mouth.

EMBARRASSMENT

For embarrassment, draw an awkward smile, eyebrows pointing upward, and short blush lines on the cheeks.

WORRY

For worry, draw a down-turned mouth with gritted teeth, raised eyebrows, and a side glance.

LAUGHTER

For laughing, open the mouth wide to show teeth and tongue, close the eyes, and add a tear.

ANGER

For anger, point the eyebrows down toward half-open eyes. The mouth is open and snarling.

SADNESS

For sadness, the eyes and eyebrows are upturned, with streams of tears below.

TIREDNESS

For tiredness, close the eyes and open the mouth wide. Yawn lines appear over the head.

LOVE

To show a character in love, make the pupils fill the eyes, add blush lines and a cute smile.

BORUTO: NARUTO NEXT GENERATIONS

The sequel to Kishimoto Masashi's ninja classic *Naruto* is a hit in its own right. Over a million copies of the manga are in the hands of fans. *Boruto: Naruto Next Generations* sees the son of the Seventh Homage Naruto lead a new team of teen trainee ninjas. But is the adventure hurtling toward a fatal finale?

BREAKDOWN

▶ **Boruto** is the son of **Uzumaki Naruto** of the **Uzumaki Clan** from **Konohagakure**—the hidden village of the Land of Fire. Already possessing considerable talent, **Boruto** undergoes training as a ninja led by **Naruto's** protégé **Sarutobi Konohamaru** and partner **Uchiha Sasuke**. When his father is kidnapped by enemies hoping to exploit the nine-tailed beast hosted by **Naruto**, **Boruto** and the ninja village leaders head out on a rescue mission. This results in **Boruto** gaining chilling new powers.

SNAPSHOT

▶ When **Kishimoto Masashi** concluded his epic manga *Naruto* in 2014, the creator was asked for a follow-up by publisher **Shueisha**. **Kishimoto** was reluctant, so instead promoted his assistant **Ikemoto Mikio** to draw what became *Boruto: Naruto Next Generations*. The son of **Naruto** had already been introduced to fans in 2015's *Boruto: Naruto The Movie*. **Kishimoto** recommended the film's co-scripter **Kodachi Ukyō** to take on the writing, too. **Kishimoto Masashi** took back the writing duties for his creation after 13 volumes of acting in a supervising role while completing a different manga series *Samurai 8: The Tale of Hachimaru.*

THE CORE
MANGA
PUBLISHED BY: Shueisha
18 volumes, 2016–
WRITERS: Kodachi Ukyō,
Kishimoto Masashi
ARTIST: Ikemoto Mikio
ANIME
PRODUCED FOR: Pierrot 2017–
WRITERS: Kodachi Ukyō, Uezu Makoto,
Honda Masaya
MOVIES
*Boruto: Naruto
the Movie* 2015

THE SEAL OF ŌTSUTSUKI

▶ After battling and defeating the malicious celestial being **Ōtsutsuki Momoshiki, Momoshiki** froze time for him and **Boruto**. He issued a warning: **"someone who defeats a god ceases to be a normal person."** He then grabbed **Boruto's** arm, leaving a **black diamond seal** imprinted on the boy's right palm. The mark is later revealed as a **Karma Seal**, which gives its bearer powers, including the abilities to fly and to absorb chakra-based ninjutsu. Using the **Karma** to its utmost threatens to transform **Boruto** into an Ōtsutsuki. **Boruto's** friend **Kawaki** bears the same seal on his left hand.

BACK TO THE FUTURE

▶ The story of **Boruto** appeared in an odd order. The first time fans got to properly meet the spiky, blond-haired shinobi on-screen after his brief debut toward the end of *The Last: Naruto the Movie* (2014) was in 2015's *Boruto: Naruto the Movie*. The manga debuted a few months afterward and began by expanding on the film's story, with **Boruto** already a genin (junior ninja). The anime TV series, which premiered in 2017, is set before the movie and manga. It tracks **Boruto** and friends' progress as they enroll at **Ninja Academy**.

FATHER ISSUES

▶ **Boruto** has a personality much like his father, **Naruto**. He's noisy, excitable, and stubborn—if a little cheekier, craftier, and more self-assured! When we meet **Boruto** in the anime, he's unhappy with his dad, who seems to be putting his role as **Seventh Hokage** ahead of his family. But, after **Boruto** witnesses his father using his abilities as a shinobi to protect the village from an attack by **Kinshiki** and **Ōtsutsuki Momoshiki**, the boy changes his mind. In the wake of **Naruto's** heroism, the pair make up. Fist bump!

TEAM 7

▶ After qualifying for the **Chūnin Exams** at **Ninja Academy**, **Boruto**, along with **Uchiha Sarada** and **Mitsuki**, are brought together as **Team 7**. The team is entrusted with missions by their sensei **Sarutobi Konohamaru**. These missions include capturing a wild bear (which they fail to do) and catching a gang of bandits that raided the Konoha Bank.

▶ **Sarada** is the daughter of **Naruto's** former teammates **Haruno Sakura** and **Uchiha Sasuke**. Like **Boruto**, **Sarada** has doubts about the role of shinobi as it kept her father away from home so much.

▶ **Mitsuki** is unusual. He's a synthetic human based on an embryo of a previous **Mitsuki**, created by his "parent," **Orochimaru**. **Mitsuki** doesn't hold back in battle and is willing to kill. But he shows a great deal of respect for his **Team 7** allies.

▶ The parents of **Boruto**, **Sarada**, and **Mitsuki** were all members of **Team 7**, too, during their time as ninja students.

FINAL COUNTDOWN

▶ A flash forward in **episode one** of the anime revealed a major confrontation between rivals **Boruto** and **Kawaki** is in the cards. The fate of **Boruto's father** is far from certain. Wanting an end to the age of the shinobi, **Kawaki** threatens to send Boruto **"where I sent the Seventh Hokage."** Does this mean straight to the afterlife? The death of a major character is not unheard of in the series. **Naruto's** host fox spirit, **Kurama**, was a major casualty in the 2021 season. It may be a while until we find out—in 2019, artist **Ikemoto** suggested it would take 30 volumes to complete the tale.

WHERE NEXT?

If you love *Boruto: Naruto Next Generations*, try:

▶ **NARUTO**
The original series is the obvious place to turn after *Boruto*. See what his dad got up to in his own ninja-training days. There are 72 volumes and 15 years of anime to catch up on!

▶ **THE LEGEND OF KORRA** (PICTURED)
A US sequel to *Avatar: The Last Airbender*, *The Legend of Korra* follows the female successor to **Aang** as she uses her element-wielding powers to deal with unrest in a modern city.

▶ **SAMURAI 8: THE TALE OF HACHIMARU**
Or check out what **Kishimoto Masahi** did before he returned to writing *Boruto*. This future-set saga follows the story of **Hachimaru**, a weakling obsessed with video games who dreams of becoming a samurai.

はい

KOMI CAN'T COMMUNICATE
(Komi-san wa, Komyushō Desu)

Komi Can't Communicate is a lighthearted, slice-of-life story about social anxiety at school. The beautiful lead character is held back by her inability to talk. There are 7.4 million copies of the award-winning manga in circulation, plus an anime and live-action TV series that aired in 2022.

BREAKDOWN

▶ Upon enrolling at Itan Private High School, **Komi Shouko** gains a lot of admirers for her beauty and elegance. But she lacks one important faculty—**the ability to talk**. **Tadano Hitohito**, the awkward schoolboy told to sit beside her, decides to make it his mission to help her. After, **Komi** expresses herself by writing on a blackboard and reveals her dream of finding one hundred friends. **Tadano** determines to help **Komi** reach her goal.

SNAPSHOT

▶ Writer/artist **Oda Tomohito** first came to prominence by picking up the grand prize for his manga *World Worst One* in the **70th Shogakukan New Comic Artist Awards** in 2012. He followed this in 2014 with *Dezicon*, the story of a troublesome schoolgirl who finds herself in control of an alien planning to take over the world. His next work, *Komi Can't Communicate*, debuted a year later as a one-shot before being picked up as a full series in 2016. **Oda** originally planned to make the main character with social anxiety male, but his editor believed a female lead would be more compelling.

THE CORE

MANGA
PUBLISHED BY: Shogakukan
27 volumes, 2016–
WRITER/ARTIST: Oda Tomohito

ANIME
PRODUCED FOR: OLM 2021–2022
WRITER: Akao Deko
24 episodes

LIVE ACTION
PRODUCED FOR: TV Man Union
2021–2022
WRITER: Mizuhashi Fumie
8 episodes

CLASSMATES

While **Komi's** difficulty in making friends is the crux of the story, other characters at the school have their own issues to deal with.

▶ **AGARI HIMIKO** is something of a **manga trope: a dandere, a timid and quiet individual** who hides away in toilet stalls. But she is slowly coming out of her shell as a friend of **Komi**.

▶ **INAKA NOKOKO** lacks **confidence and struggles to make friends**. Perhaps she feels out of sorts as a country girl with a rural accent who is thrust into the big city.

▶ **SHISUTO NARUSE** is **not** short of confidence. He's convinced that everyone must be his admirer, including **Komi**. Only thing is, he seriously lacks self-awareness and is very clumsy.

▶ **OTORI KAEDE** is a **daydreamer** who is **easily distracted** and can get lost if not supervised.

BLOSSOMING ROMANCE

▶ While **Tadano Hitohito** has busied himself expanding **Komi's** friendship circle, his low self-esteem has prevented him from pursuing anything more than a platonic relationship with **Komi**. For fans of the manga and anime, it's clear that **Komi** has strong feelings for her first friend at the school and would love to take it further. What is the chance of both characters finally expressing themselves fully before long?

SILENT SCREEN

▶ Appearing on Japanese screens just one month ahead of the anime adaptation, the live-action version of *Komi Can't Communicate* seems to have failed to make the grade. Only one season of eight episodes surfaced. The show starred **Ikeda Eraiza** (PICTURED) as **Komi Shouko** and 35-year-old Jpop star **Masuda Takahisa** as **Tadano Hitohito**.

GENDER BALANCE

▶ Among the cast of *Komi Can't Communicate* is one interesting and popular addition, the very communicative **Osana Najimi**. Osana is introduced by **Tadano** to **Komi** as a girl, but he later remembers they wore a male uniform through middle school. **Osana** uses the pronoun "boku" to describe themself.

This word can be applied to either male or female in Japan. While the confusion over gender is used as a source of humor, the introduction of a key **gender-fluid character** in a school setting is a breakthrough for manga and anime—especially because it doesn't define **Osana**. Instead, their main characteristic is being a loyal friend.

TO BE CONTINUED?

▶ The second season of *Komi Can't Communicate* welcomed several new characters to add to **Komi's** list of friends, including **Katai Makoto**. On the outside, he appears to be the typical beefed-up schoolboy troublemaker, but we soon learn he's a softie inside. In some ways, he is the male equivalent of Komi—outwardly impressive but struggling to find ways to express affection. The contradiction of **Makoto's** looks and personality mark him up as a classic "gap moe" character. **Tadano** is one of the first at Itan to befriend **Makoto**, and he soon joins the circle with **Komi**.

▶ Meanwhile, **Komi** is making progress and is able to mingle without **Tadano** or **Najimi** nudging her along. She managed to open up to **Katou Mikuni** and **Sasaki Ayami** on a school trip.

WHERE NEXT?

If you love *Komi Can't Communicate*, try:

▶ **HORIMIYA**
Comedy with kindhearted classmates and a slow-building romance are the core of this anime. We see the male lead, **Hachiōji Naoto**, struggling to overcome his natural shyness.

▶ **SENRYU GIRL** (PICTURED)
Senryu Girl is a manga and short-lived anime, and its plot is similar to *Komi*. It follows a **silent schoolgirl** who communicates only through a chalkboard. The protagonist, **Yukishiro Nanako**, uses poetry to describe her feelings.

▶ **A SILENT VOICE**
Another shy girl, another high school. Here it's **Nishimiya Shōko**, who is deaf. She is helped by her classmate **Ishida Shoya**—a former bully hoping to make amends for his past behavior.

MOBILE SUIT GUNDAM
(Kidō Senshi Gundam)

Mobile Suit Gundam was a groundbreaking anime. It took the classic super-robot trope and then fit it within a vast sci-fi saga packed with well-rounded characters. It spawned a huge market in collectable models, launched the Real Robot genre, and paved the way for armies of mecha manga and movies.

BREAKDOWN

▶ In the **Universal Century year 0079**, the colony of **Zeon** launched a war for independence against the **Earth Federation**. With their **giant human-shaped robot technology** (the **Zaku mobile suits**), Zeon inflicted huge damage on Earth and its supporting space settlements during its **One Year War**, wiping out half of humanity.

▶ When the **planet Side 7** is attacked by Zeon, the teenager **Amuro Ray** commandeers a prototype **RX-78-2 Gundam mobile suit** to force them back. Having impressed embattled **Federation defenders** with his piloting skills, **Amuro** is brought aboard the *White Base* battleship led by the commander **Bright Noah**. Crewed by a mix of soldiers and civilian refugees, the *White Base* faces a continuing battle against the **Zeon** forces led by **Lieutenant Commander Char Aznable** (the "Red Comet") as it strives to deliver the **RX-78** to Earth.

RX-78-2

▶ The **Gundam prototype** piloted by **Amuro Ray** was the second of three built in secret on **Side 7** as a response to **Zeon's** mass-produced mobile suit, the **MS-06 Zaku II**. The mobile suits were part of **Operation V**, a defense project led by **Tem Ray, Amuro's** father.

▶ The **Earth Federation RX-78-2's Luna titanium alloy shell** was lighter than **Zeon** tech. The prototype carried major firepower including a beam rifle, plasma sabers, hyper bazooka and hammer, plus a **large defensive shield**. The success of the **RX-78-2** led to the mass production of the **RGM-79 GM**. After its destruction in battle, the **RX-78-2** was succeeded by the **Gundam Mk-II, Zeta Gundam,** and **ZZ Gundam**.

THE CORE

MANGA

PUBLISHED BY: Akita Shoten
WRITER/ARTIST: Okazaki Yū
2 volumes

ANIME

PRODUCED FOR: Nippon Sunrise, 1979–1980
WRITER: Tomino Yoshiyuki
43 episodes, plus 3 movies
edited from the episodes:
Mobile Suit Gundam I 1981
Mobile Suit Gundam II:
Soldiers of Sorrow 1981
Mobile Suit Gundam III: Encounters
in Space 1982

NEWTYPE

▶ There is more to the young **Amuro Ray** than first appears. As his adventures progress, he discovers he is a **Newtype**, which is a human born with exceptional mental abilities. This evolution is understood to be the result of humankind adapting to life off Earth.

SAVED BY TOYS

▶ The initial run of 52 episodes of *Mobile Suit Gundam* was cut back to 39 due to its poor initial reception. (It was later extended to 43.) While the show struggled to pull in viewers at first, **toys** based on the mobile suits were a **massive success**. In the wake of merchandise sales, the show was revived! Three movies were culled from the TV anime for cinema release and helped to continue the concept to this day.

LOVESTRUCK

▶ **Amuro** meets and falls in love with a **Newtype** like himself. **Lalah Sune** had been rescued by **Amuro's** mortal enemy, **Char**, and employed as a pilot for his mobile armor "Elmeth." During battle with **Char**, **Amuro** accidentally kills **Lalah**. A final battle between **Amuro Ray** and the **"Red Comet"** at the **Fortress of A Baoa Qu** takes place. Both combatants blame the other for **Lalah's** death, making for a dramatic and emotional series finale.

QUALITY CONTROL

▶ Series creator **Tomino Yoshiyuki** requested that episode 15, "Cucuruz Doan's Island," be denied international release. He felt the episode didn't match the quality of the rest of the series. As the second country to air *Mobile Suit Gundam*, Italy is the only place outside Japan to have broadcast all 43 original episodes.

REAL-G

As part of the 30th anniversary of *Gundam,* a life-size animated mobile suit named **Real-G** was built in a park in Tokyo, Japan, in 2009. The 59-foot-tall mecha attracted **4.15 million visitors** before being relocated to Odaiba, where it stood until 2016.

THE LEGACY CONTINUES

▶ Three **Gundam** manga series have been published since the anime launched in 1979. The first was written by **Okazaki Yū** from 1979 to 1980, and the second by **Kondo Kazuhisa** (*Mobile Suit Gundam 0079*) from 1993 to 2005. *Mobile Suit Gundam: The Origin* (PICTURED) by **Yasuhiko Yoshikazu** ran from 2001 to 2011. A sequel to *Mobile Suit Gundam 0079* titled *Episode II Luna* is now being serialized in the monthly Japanese magazine *Gundam Ace*.

RISE OF THE REAL ROBOT

▶ *Mobile Suit Gundam* inspired a new genre in manga and anime, **Real Robots**. As opposed to the **Super Robots**, like **Gigantor** (Tetsujin 28-go, 1956) and **Mazinger Z** (1972), **Real Robots** were more realistic, human-operated armor. **Gundam** creators led the way, with mech designer **Ōkawara Kunio** working on the suits for *Fang of the Sun Dougram* (1981), while **Gundam** writer **Tomino Yoshiyuki** came up with **Combat Mecha Xabungle** in 1982.

▶ Outside of the **Gundam** franchise, the biggest mecha hitters include Kawamori Shōji's *Robotech* (PICTURED) (1982) and Hideaki Anno's *Neon Genesis Evangelion* (1995).

FAIRY TAIL
(Fearī Teiru)

A lighthearted, time-twisting, and action-packed romp through a world of fantasy, *Fairy Tail* features a familiar cast of wizards, knights, and dragon slayers, plus a catlike comedy sidekick. The saga ran for an impressive 11 years and had a host of spin-offs, plus an anime series, OVAs, two movies, and several video games.

BREAKDOWN

▶ **Dragon Slayer Natsu Dragneel** from the **Fairy Tail guild** is on a quest to find his adoptive father, a dragon named **Igneel**, along with his blue feline sidekick, **Happy**. The journey takes him across Earth-land's **Kingdom of Fiore**, where he is joined by a young female wannabe guild wizard named **Lucy Heartfilia**, ice mage **Gray Fullbuster**, and knight **Ezra Scarlet**. Together **Team Natsu** face many challenges, including dark guilds, demons, and a magically immortal and evil wizard.

SNAPSHOT

▶ **Mashima Hiro** got his manga break after winning a competition for his one-shot *Magician* in 1998. His first major published work was *Rave Master*—the story of a teenager on a quest to find five pieces of a sacred stone. *Rave Master* lasted for six years and was adapted for the anime *Groove Adventure Rave* in 2001. For the follow-up, *Fairy Tail*, **Mashima** wanted to write a fantasy that was like a party, where characters come together to find their vocation and have fun. Since the end of *Fairy Tail*, **Mashima** has been working on sequels and a new shōnen series, *Edens Zero*, which he is developing into video games.

THE CORE

MANGA

PUBLISHED BY: Kondansha
63 volumes, 2006–2017
WRITER/ARTIST: Mashima Hiro
SPIN-OFFS: *Fairy Tail Zero* 2014–2015
Fairy Tail: 100 Years Quest 2018–

ANIME

PRODUCED FOR: A1 Studios, Satelight, Bridge, CloverWorks 2009–2019
WRITER: Sogo Masashi
328 episodes

MOVIES

9 OVAs
Fairy Tail the Movie: Phoenix Priestess 2012
Fairy Tail: Dragon Cry 2017

TAIL OR TALE

▶ **Mashima** tested the water for his fantasy epic with a one-shot called *Fairy Tale* in 2002, where the hero, **Natsu**, was a fire-wielding member of a guild of couriers. Four years later, he reconsidered this setup for a long-running saga and made **Natsu** a Dragon Slayer from a wizard guild. He also changed the title to *Fairy Tail*, with the tail supposedly belonging to a fairy. **Mashima** teased that the **"tail"** might be an important plot point . . .

PREQUEL, SEQUEL

▶ The original manga *Fairy Tail* ended in 2017. But **Mashima** expanded the premise with both a prequel, *Fairy Tail Zero*, and a sequel, *Fairy Tail: 100 Years Quest* (PICTURED), for which he provided rough layouts for the artist **Ueda Atsuo** to follow. There have been several spin-offs, including *Fairy Tail: Ice Trail, Fairy Tail: Blue Mistral, Fairy Girls, Fairy Tail Garden, Fairy Tail: Happy's Heroic Adventure,* and *Fairy Tail City Hero*. Several crossovers between **Mashima's** characters have also been published, including 2019's *Mashima's Hero's*, which stars characters from *Fairy Tail, Rave Master,* and *Edens Zero*. It's a quest just to find them all!

HAPPY NOW?

▶ One of the best-loved characters in *Fairy Tail* is **Happy**, **Natsu's** companion. He appears to be a **talking blue cat**, but he's actually an Exceed from **Extalia** who can also transform. He sprouts feathered wings to carry passengers much larger and heavier than himself for a brief while. As his name suggests, he's a jolly little fellow who is happy in the company of others and keen to help. Yup!

GAME FOR IT

▶ **Mashima's** work has been adapted for several video games—a platform the creator seems eager to be involved in. Twelve console and app titles have been released for *Fairy Tail* alone—from the combat game *Fairy Tail Portable Guild* to the more-recent RPG, *Fairy Tail* (2020). **Mashima** is working on a new RPG for *Edens Zero* featuring the characters **Rebecca Bluegarden** and **Happy**.

WELL-ROUNDED VILLAINS

▶ One of the most important elements of **Mashima's** storytelling is the creation of believable villains, with understandable motivations. Both *Rave Master's* **Lucia** and *Fairy Tail's* **Zeref** are not simply black-and-white adversaries. **Zeref Dragneel** is **Natsu's** magically immortal older brother. He's one of the strongest known mages who was the former emperor of the **Alvarez Empire**, and is cursed to take life from those around him. Though hundreds of years old, he appears youthful. His connection with **Natsu** is more complex than a mere bloodline and involves resurrection and a death wish.

FAIRY TAIL IN SPACE

▶ A boy, a girl, and a talking cat named **Happy** head out on a quest. But this is not *Fairy Tail*. *Edens Zero* is **Mashima Hiro's** latest epic, and it's a manga and anime set in space. Here **Happy** is a robot (the spitting image of the Earth-land kitty), and he's part of the warship *Edens Zero* crew, along with **Shiki Granbell**, the grandson of **Demon King Ziggy**, and **B-Cuber Rebecca Bluegarden**. Following a robot rebellion, the trio head to the stars in search of a legendary space goddess called Mother. The manga is still going at 24 volumes and counting! A second season of the anime adaptation is due in 2023.

WHERE NEXT?

If you love *Fairy Tail*, try:

▶ **THE SEVEN DEADLY SINS** (PICTURED)
A **deposed princess** leads a quest to recruit a group of **seven powerful knights** to reclaim her realm from evil tyrants while stopping them from unleashing the fearsome **Demon Clan**.

▶ **INUYASHA**
A schoolgirl falls through a magic well and lands in feudal-era Japan. There, she meets the **heroic half-human-half-dog demon Inuyasha**. Together they seek the pieces of a magical gemstone before it can be claimed by an evil demon.

▶ **RAVE MASTER**
Mashima Hiro's previous work follows a similar plot to *Fairy Tail*, with a young male protagonist, **Haru Glory**. **Haru** is joined by a quirky bunch of allies who help him find the pieces of a magical stone that can help him defeat a demon.

DEMON SLAYER
(Kimetsu no Yaiba)

One of the top 10 best-selling manga titles of all time, *Demon Slayer* has sold over 102 million copies. This is a tale of revenge in Taishō-era Japan. It follows a young boy seeking to cure his demonized sister by collecting the blood of an army of demons.

BREAKDOWN

▶ In early 20th-century Japan, teenager **Kamado Tanjirō** is one of the only survivors of a demon attack on a mountain village. His family was killed and his sister, **Nezuko**, transformed into a demon. Seeking vengeance, **Tanjirō** trains to be a **demon slayer**. On graduating to the **Demon Slayer Corps**, the boy begins hunting down demons to restore his sister's humanity. But to create a cure, **Tanjirō** needs to collect the blood of the **Twelve Kizuki**—the strongest demons used by the powerful demon **Muzan**.

SNAPSHOT

▶ *Demon Slayer* followed several attempts by the artist **Gotōge Koyoharu** to create a long-running manga serial. Inspired by *Gintama*, *JoJo's Bizarre Adventure*, *Naruto*, *Bleach*, and *Berserk*, **Gotōge** developed the swords-and-demons saga *Kisatsu no Nagare*. It was rejected for being too dark and serious in tone, so he revised the pitch. **Gotōge** gave it a new title, *Kimetsu no Yaiba*, which means "*Blade of Demon Destruction*." The manga was given the title *Demon Slayer* in Western markets. Following the conclusion of *Demon Slayer*, **Gotōge** is said to be working on a sci-fi romantic comedy.

THE CORE

MANGA
PUBLISHED BY: Shueisha
23 volumes, 2016–2020
WRITER/ARTIST: Gotōge Koyoharu

ANIME
PRODUCED BY: Ufotable, 2019–
WRITER: Ufotable
44 episodes

MOVIES
Demon Slayer: Kimetsu no Yaiba – The Movie: Mugen Train 2020

THE MARK

▶ **Tanjirō** bears the **Mark of a Demon Slayer** on his face. First displayed by **Yoriichi Tsugikuni**, the strongest of the **Demon Slayers**, the Mark is gifted to members of the **Demon Slayer Corps**. The Mark can be awakened and change in size and appearance. **Tanjirō's** mark takes on a flame-like pattern. The Mark enhances the speed and strength of the bearer. It allows him or her to see into the "Transparent World" and observe a foe's blood and breathing movements to predict their next actions.

SLAYER SISTER

▶ At the heart of *Demon Slayer* is the sibling relationship between **Tanjirō** and **Nezuko**. **Tanjirō** will do his utmost to protect his younger sister— and she also acts to defend him! She can do so with **augmented demon powers** that allow her to grow larger, gain superstrength, heal at astonishing speed, and change into an enhanced horned demon form. To stop herself from biting humans and spreading the demon curse, she chooses to wear a **bamboo muzzle**. Like all demons, **Nezuko** is, initially, vulnerable to sunlight.

DEMON HEAD

▶ **Kibutsuji Muzan** is the cunning and merciless **Demon King** who is leader of the **Twelve Kizuki** and responsible for the attack on **Tanjirō's** village. **Muzan** was turned into a demon through an experiment that was meant to cure his terminal illness a thousand years ago. He's since shared his blood and created an army of demons under his control. **Muzan** is a dapper dresser—think fedoras and tuxedos! But he can alter his appearance dramatically to take on the body of a woman or a child, or even a combat form with extended spiked and fanged arms, or nine-bladed back whips.

THE BREATHING STYLE

▶ **Kamado Tanjirō** is a master of the Breathing Style of swordfighting. As taught by the **Demon Slayer Corps**, Breathing Styles replicate natural elements—like fire, water, and wind— guiding the movements of **Demon Slayers**. **Tanjirō** initially used a Water Breathing technique, following his mentor **Urokodaki Sakonji**. This Breathing Style has 11 forms and helps **Tanjirō** fight with fluid motions. **Tanjirō** later discovered the rare ability to combine more than one technique. **Tanjirō's** allies, **Agatsuma Zenitsu, Inosuke Hashibira**, and **Tsuyuri Kanao** are adept at Thunder, Beast, and Flower Breathing Styles.

STAGE SHOW

Demon Slayer was adapted for two stage plays that ran in Japanese theaters in 2020 and 2022. The plays were written and directed by **Suemitsu Kenichi**, with **Wada Shunsuke** providing the music.

BEING BOARING

▶ One of the more curious-looking members of **Tanjirō's Demon Slayer Corps** is **Hashibira Inosuke**. He insists on wearing a hollowed-out boar's head in honor of his late adoptive boar mother. Some work was required on the eyes to allow **Inosuke** to see where he's going and whom he's fighting. Like a wild pig, **Inosuke** is short-tempered and defensive. Having been brought up by boars, Inosuke struggles at first to understand and collaborate with his human allies.

SWORDSMITH SEASON

▶ A third season of the anime *Demon Slayer* has been promised for 2023. It is set to cover the **Swordsmith Village arc**—the ninth story line from the manga. This sees **Tanjirō** seek out **Haganezuka Hotaru**, the smith who forged his sword, to repair it while demons close in. The new episodes are due to premiere in April 2023 in a one-hour special. The whole cast is returning, along with director **Sotozaki Haruo**, and the character designer and chief animation director **Matsushima Akira**.

WHERE NEXT?

If you love *Demon Slayer*, try:

▶ **BLUE EXORCIST** (PICTURED)
For another quest to defeat a **demon king**, check out *Blue Exorcist*. On finding out he is the son of **Satan**, **Rin** joins the **True Cross Academy** to train and take on his diabolical father. But he risks coming under the devil's influence.

▶ **YU YU HAKUSHO**
A '90s classic, *Yu Yu Hakusho* is the story of a kindhearted teen delinquent, **Hakusho**. He is brought back from the dead by spirits to join a team of demons solving supernatural crimes.

▶ **JUJUTSU KAISEN**
If you simply can't get enough demons, try *Jujutsu Kaisen*. It's the story of **Itadori Yūji**, a boy who swallows a cursed demon finger (yuck!) and becomes cursed himself. To remove the curse, he needs to locate the rest of the demon's divided body.

TORIYAMA AKIRA

Toriyama Akira has become an inspiration for generations of mangaka as the creator of one of the world's most successful and influential manga and anime works, *Dragon Ball*. The adventures of Son Goku continue to be an international sensation in books, on-screen, and in video games.

BREAKDOWN

▶ **Toriyama Akira** was born in 1955 in Nagoya, Japan. He was first drawn into the world of manga by a school friend's collection of **Tezuka Osamu's** *Astro Boy* (page 112). After finishing school, **Toriyama** designed posters for advertising before submitting samples of his manga to publishers. His first pitch was a *Star Wars* parody that sadly got turned down. But in 1978, with encouragement from editors, he came up with *Wonder Island*—his first published work. It was not a hit, but **Toriyama** didn't give up and he turned in *Dr. Slump* a year later. This funny tale of a small, superpowered girl robot was a huge hit, but nothing on the scale of his next series. *Dragon Ball* is a manga, anime, game, and merchandising juggernaut and **one of the most successful titles of all time!**

WIND-UP

Toriyama Akira included a caricature of himself in *Dr. Slump*. He portrayed himself as **Tori**, a wind-up blue bird carrying a huge pencil. **Tori** means **"bird"** in Japanese.

DR. SLUMP

▶ It may be less known internationally than *Dragon Ball*, but *Dr. Slump* was **Toriyama's** first major work, and it was a major success in Japan. It's set in **Penguin Village** where humans and talking animals coexist. *Dr. Slump* stars as an eccentric professor named Norimaki Senbē (also known as Dr. Slump) and the invention he tries to pass off as a relative—the superstrong and naïve robot girl, **Arale**. *Dr. Slump* is filled with playful comedy, puns, and toilet humor. There are guest appearances

and characters who regularly break the fourth wall. It was the hit **Toriyama** needed to launch his career as an imaginative mangaka. The manga was published by *Weekly Shōnen Jump* from 1980 to 1984. It was adapted for two anime series, *Dr. Slump & Arale-chan* (1981–1986) and *Doctor Slump* (1997–1999). Eleven *Dr. Slump* anime movies were released between 1981 and 2007, proving the lasting popularity of the characters.

DRAGON BALL

▶ It's hard to overestimate what a huge hit *Dragon Ball* became. It was **Torishima Kazuhiko** (**Toriyama's** editor at **Shueisha**) who suggested the writer and artist be inspired by his love of **kung fu movies** to create an action-packed shōnen manga. **Toriyama** came up with the two-part *Dragon Boy* in 1983, about **Tangtong**, a boy with martial-arts skills who protects a princess on her journey home. This was the foundation for *Dragon Ball*. The princess was dropped, **Tangtong** became **Son Goku**, and a quest for dragon-raising spheres was launched.

▶ *Dragon Ball* debuted in *Weekly Shōnen Jump* in 1984. The series shared a lot of the humor of *Dr. Slump* in its early days, but it became more action focused as **Goku** matured in later chapters, with **Torishima's** art turning more angular and the battles more serious.

▶ The popularity of *Dragon Ball* propelled sales of *Weekly Shōnen Jump* to an all-time high of 6.53 million copies in 1995. Over an 11-year run, **Torishima** completed 519 chapters collected in 42 volumes. This led to five anime adaptations, 21 animated movies, a live-action film, and countless video games. As a brand, *Dragon Ball* took off far beyond Japan, with 350 million copies of the manga sold and continuing to be sold in Asia, Europe, and the Americas.

GOKU'S JOURNEY

▶ *Dragon Ball* was inspired by the 16th-century Chinese tale **Journey to the West** (known as Saiyuki in Japan). This included a monkey hero named **Son Wukong** joining a monk's quest across China and India in search of sacred scrolls. **Toriyama** kept the monkey tail for his hero **Son Goku**, and had him seeking seven magical orbs, which together could summon a powerful dragon.

HAPPY GOKU DAY

▶ May 9 is officially **Goku Day** in Japan. In 2015, the Japan Anniversary Association celebrated the long-running manga by introducing an annual event. But why this date? In Japanese, the numbers five and nine can be pronounced as "Go" and "Ku," hence 5/9!

THE TORIYAMA-VERSE

▶ **Toriyama** had **Dragon Ball's Goku** visit **Penguin Village** in the *General Blue Saga* (manga volume 7) with **Norimaki Arale** eagerly joining **Goku** in taking on the **Red Ribbon Army**. Arale also appeared in several *Dragon Ball Z* video games, and as a playable character in 2007's *Dragon Ball Budōkai Tenkaichi 3*, before reappearing in the anime *Dragon Ball Super*

(PICTURED) in 2016. Other **Toriyama** characters that earned cameos in the world of *Dragon Ball* includes **Neko Majin Z**—a bizarre cat creature from *Nekomajin* (an occasional *Dragon Ball* parody series **Toriyama** worked on between 1999 and 2005), and **Jaco the Galactic Patrolman** from the 2013–2014 **Toriyama** manga of the same name.

HE WILL CONTINUE ON TO THE TENKAICHI BUDOUKAI !!

YAA-AAY!!

STRONGEST UNDER THE HEAVENS

▶ A staple of the *Dragon Ball* series is the training competition Tenkaichi Budōkai or **"Strongest Under the Heavens Martial Arts Tournament"** on Papaya Island, where **Goku** and his allies return after their periodic quests for **Dragon Balls**. The first tournament proved to be one of the most engaging elements of the series and saw a spike in interest in *Dragon Ball*. From then on, the focus of the manga became the battles rather than the quests—something that carried over to the many *Dragon Ball* video games.

MANGA AND ANIME

RECORD BREAKERS

Western comics and TV shows can only dream of the sales figures of Japanese manga! The mangaka and assistants work round the clock to deliver world-beating, weekly chapters of fan favorites. Anime has also produced some real record breakers, with thousands of episodes of popular shows being aired over decades and box-office-beating movies. Here are some of the astounding stats . . .

ONE PIECE

BEST-SELLING MANGA

▶ The **number-one best-selling manga title of all time** is *One Piece* (see page 12). Of the 104 volumes published so far, each has an average of **4.97 million** sold. Adding up the sales of all copies in circulation comes to an estimated **516.6 million**! That's enough for everyone in the United States to have 1.5 copies each!

Of those **516.6 million** copies, about **416 million** were picked up in Japan, and **100 million** picked up in 60 countries outside Japan. That's a massive international success for **Monkey D. Luffy** and his crew!

GOLGO 13

LONGEST-RUNNING MANGA

▶ The adventures of assassin-for-hire **Golgo 13** have been running with very little interruption (just two months off due to 2020 Covid restrictions) since its debut in the Japanese manga *Big Comic* in October 1968. Sadly, the series creator **Saitō Takao** passed away in 2021. Following his wishes, the editorial team at **Saito Production** have kept the hits coming. If you want to read from the start, you have **207 tankōbon** and **563 chapters** to catch up on. As a result of its longevity, *Golgo 13* is the **third top-selling** manga title and **biggest-selling seinen manga series** in history!

DORAEMON

MOST ANIME EPISODES

▶ The lovable **time-traveling robot cat** *Doraemon* (page 174) made the leap from manga to anime in April 1973. The show has been produced by many different studios since its debut and is still going to this day. Over its **40-year** TV history, **3,070 episodes** have been made. This includes **26 TV episodes** from the original series, **1,787** from the 1979 series, and **1,160** from the 2005 series, plus **30 special episodes**, **40 feature films**, **two special films**, **14 short films**, **four** *Dorami-chan* movies, **two** *Dorami-chan* and *Doraemons* films, and **five** *The Doraemons* films. Phew!

SOREIKE! ANPANMAN

MOST ANIME CHARACTERS

▶ **Yanase Takashi** created the long-running manga *Anpanman* back in 1973. **Fifteen years** later, it was adapted into a hugely popular anime for young Japanese children, *Soreike! Anpanman (Let's Go! Anpanman)*. **Anpanman** is a superhero with an ansan (red-bean-paste pastry) head who defends the planet from the evil germ **Baikinman**. While little known internationally, **Anpanman** is a higher-grossing character than *Hello Kitty* in Japan. He even has a **BTS song** named after him!

ISHINOMORI SHOTARO

MOST PUBLISHED AUTHOR

▶ Known as **"The King of Manga,"** Ishinomori Shōtarō is the creator of *Cyborg 009*, *Kamen Rider*, and *Super Sentai* (which is as internationally famous as *Power Rangers*). Born in 1938, **Ishinomori** began his manga career in 1954 with the title *Nikyuu Tenshi* before joining the legend **Tezuka Osamu** (see page 108) as an assistant on *Astro Boy*. Sadly, **Ishinomori** died just days after his 60th birthday. Nine years later, he was awarded the record for the **most comics** published by one author. His total adds up to an astounding **128,000 pages** across **770 titles** in **500 volumes**.

SAZAE-SAN

LONGEST-RUNNING ANIME

▶ While there are more episodes of *Doraemon* in existence, the show first appeared in 1973. Beating it by four years as the official **longest-running animated show** is *Sazae-San*, which debuted in 1969 and continues to this day (interrupted for just one month in 2020). The lighthearted comedy series tells the story of **Sazae-San** and her family and was launched as a manga by **Hasegawa Machiko** in 1946. It ran until 1974, but it is the anime that has proved the most enduring.

ATTACK ON TITAN

LARGEST COMIC BOOK

▶ **Isayama Hajime's** *Attack on Titan* (Shingeki no Kyojin) is a hugely popular shōnen manga. It features a human race struggling to survive against gigantic, man-eating Titans. Fittingly, this tale of behemoths was celebrated with the **largest-ever comic book** in 2021. Measuring **39 x 28 in (100 x 70.3 cm)** this special edition of the 35th volume in the series is not something you'd pack to read on the train. The mega-manga weighs **30.3 lb (13.75 kg)**—that's about 36 times the size of a regular *Attack on Titan* volume. One hundred copies were printed and soon sold out!

THE TALE OF THE PRINCESS KAGUYA

MOST EXPENSIVE ANIME

▶ The 2013 animated historical fantasy *The Tale of the Princess Kaguya* is not only the most-expensive Japanese animated movie but the **most-expensive Japanese movie** of any kind. Directed by **Takahata Isao** for **Studio Ghibli** (see page 72), the movie cost **5 billion yen (US $49.3 million)** to produce. **Takahata** was a meticulous creator who never rushed. The movie was announced in 2008.

DEMON SLAYER THE MOVIE: MUGEN TRAIN

HIGHEST-GROSSING ANIME MOVIE

▶ The *Demon Slayer (Kimetsu no Yaiba)* anime series (see page 54) big-screen adventure was **Japan's biggest-earning movie** of 2020 and the **highest-grossing Japanese movie** of all time. Naturally this means it's also the **biggest-earning anime movie** of all time. Released during the pandemic, *Mugen Train* earned more than **US $506.5 million** worldwide.

KINGDOM

MOST CREATORS ON ONE MANGA

▶ Japanese manga is rare in that it generally continues with one writer/artist at the helm for decades. To keep up with the busy schedules, most artists use assistants to fill in backgrounds, though. At the other extreme is a record-breaking attempt to have the **most creators working on one strip**.

▶ On December 12, 2012, the publishers **Shueisha** organized an online event for **Hara Yasuhisa's** historic manga *Kingdom*. They invited **1,087 amateur and professional artists** to redraw a panel from the title's 26th volume that they described as "Social Kingdom." Among those who got involved were *One Piece's* **Oda Eiichirō**, *Naruto's* **Kishimoto Masashi**, and *JoJo's Bizarre Adventure's* **Araki Hirohiko**. The book has only appeared online, however.

FRUITS BASKET

(Furūtsu Basuketto)

Fruits Basket at first appears to be a shōjo staple. It has a super-friendly lead dealing with loss, who is confused by social graces and making new friends. But then it thrusts its young protagonist, Honda Tōru, into the world of zodiac spirits with a family cursed to transform into animals. Over time, this apparent comedy aspect is overshadowed by the implications of the curse and the stress it puts on the relationships in the clan.

BREAKDOWN

▶ When **Honda Tōru's** mother dies in a traffic accident, she moves in with her grandfather. During house renovations, **Tōru** opts to move out and live in a tent. She camps on land that turns out to owned by the **Sōma family**. When a landslide destroys her tent, the family invite her to move indoors. By accident, she discovers the clan are possessed by a curse that changes them into **Chinese zodiac animals** when stressed or hugged by the opposite sex. Generous **Tōru** is determined to help her new friends deal with their emotional struggles with the **jinx** and eventually meets the spirits that control the curse. Through her efforts **Tōru** learns much about her own life.

SNAPSHOT

▶ **Takaya Natsuki's** professional debut was the tale *Born Free*, published in *Hana to Yume* magazine in 1992. This was followed by *Phantom Dream*, a fantasy romance published from 1994 to 1997. It included subjects that would reemerge in *Fruits Basket*, such as maleficent spirits and abusive parents. **Takaya** followed *Phantom Dream* (PICTURED) with the postapocalyptic romance *Tsubasa: Those with Wings*, but it was 1998's *Fruits Basket* that made her name. Hers became one of the best-selling shōjo manga and landed a 2001 **Kodansha Manga Award**.

THE CORE

MANGA
PUBLISHED BY: Hakusensha
23 volumes, 1998–2006
WRITER/ARTIST: Takaya Natsuki

ANIME
PRODUCED FOR: Studio Teen, 2001
WRITER: Higuchi Tachibana
89 episodes

MOVIES
Fruits Basket: Prelude 2022

WHY "FRUITS BASKET"?

▶ The title comes from a kids' game, where children sit in a ring and take the names of fruit. When a fruit is called out, the child claiming that name has to get up and rush to find a new seat in the circle. Playing the game at school, **Tōru** was made to feel excluded by other children who named her "rice ball," so she never got chosen. Just as **Tōru** was isolated by bullies at school, so the cursed **Sōma family** are set apart from society. And, yes, the correct translation would be **"Fruit Basket,"** but no one cared to fix it.

LEGEND OF THE ZODIAC

▶ *Fruits Basket* is inspired by the Chinese **legend of the zodiac** when animals were invited to join a feast laid out by a god. All the animals that attended had a year named after them. The **rat** tricked the **cat** into believing the feast was a later day, leaving the animal out of the group. **Tōru** had been told the story of the zodiac by her mother and felt sympathy for the plight of the **cat**. She wished she had been born in the Year of the **Cat** rather than the **Dog**.

RAT VS. CAT

▶ One of **Tōru's** first encounters with the **Sōma family** is with her classmate **Sōma Yuki** and his orange-haired cousin **Kyo**. The pair are at odds, just as the animals they are possessed by—the **rat** and **cat**. It is **Tōru's** grabbing of **Kyo** during the fight that reveals the family's secret.

PARENTHOOD

▶ Parental figures in *Fruits Basket* are not the best role models. **Akito**, the female head of the **Sōma clan**, is one of the most disturbing of all. Having been emotionally abused by her mother, **Akito** was forced into being raised as a boy.

Akito was possessed by the zodiac's god spirit and began to assert control over the zodiac animal spirits. Both needy and cruel, she became a twisted creature, mistreating family members such as **Yuki** and **Kisa**.

The revelation that **Akito** was a woman who was brought up as a boy appeared too late in the manga for the first anime adaptation in 2001. The TV series portrayed **Akito** as a man throughout. The 2019 adaptation corrected this.

ANOTHER HARVEST

▶ **Takaya Natsuki** launched a sequel, *Fruits Basket Another* in 2015. This did not feature any of the key characters— **Tohru**, **Yuki**, or **Kyo**—from the original manga. It was followed by a spin-off *The Three Musketeers Arc* in 2019, which focused on the so-called **Mabudachi Trio of Sōma Ayame, Sōma Hatori**, and **Sōma Shigure**.

GAME FOR IT

▶ The 2022 anime movie *Fruits Basket: Prelude* acted as a recap for the 2019 series. It also featured a story set before the events in the series. **Honda Tōru's parents** appeared, plus a new epilogue starring **Tōru** and **Kyo** that was written by **Takaya Natsuki**.

WHERE NEXT?

If you love *Fruits Basket*, try:

▶ **KAMISAMA KISS**

As with *Fruits Basket*'s **Honda Tōru, Momozono Nanami** is a homeless high school student who moves in with an unusual new family. In this case, home is a shrine, where **Nanami** begins to fall for the familiar of an **earth deity**.

▶ **VAMPIRE KNIGHT** (PICTURED)

Fans of the *Twilight* franchise will be on familiar territory with *Vampire Knight*. **Yuki Ross** is the daughter of the school headmaster. She links up with handsome vampires after dark, getting caught up in a secret world of romance and danger.

▶ **RANMA 1/2**

A hit from the vaults, this 1989 anime features **Tendō Akane**. She's a tomboy engaged to **Ranma**—a male martial-arts hero who transforms into a girl when splashed by water. Many other characters turn back and forth into animals, too.

TOWER OF GOD

(Kami no Tou)

As a webtoon, South Korean manhwa *Tower of God* has reached a phenomenal number of readers. All are eager to follow the progress of its young hero and comrades who slowly advance through the levels of a mysterious tower. If someone reaches the highest level, their desires are granted.

BREAKDOWN

▶ A young boy known as **Twenty-Fifth Bam** has spent most of his life trapped in a dark cave beneath a structure known as **the Tower** with his friend **Rachel**. When **Rachel** gets out, **Bam** is desperate to find her and manages to enter **the Tower. The Tower** features many levels with different inhabitants and magical properties. To reach the top, **Bam** faces a quick learning curve to pass tests of strength and intelligence while building new friendships.

SNAPSHOT

▶ **Lee Jong-hui**, known by his pen-name **SIU**, studied art before military service in South Korea. On the advice of an older recruit, **SIU** began drawing the comics that became the basis for his webtoon *Tower of God*. With eight years of story mapped out, **SIU** began sharing his epic in 2010, and he shows no sign of slowing down more than 12 years later. The manhwa has been translated into 28 languages and received over 4.5 billion views worldwide, with an RPG game and anime adaptation to boot.

THE CORE
MANHWA
PUBLISHED BY: Naver Webtoon
11 volumes, 2010–
WRITER/ARTIST: SIU (Lee Jong-hui)
ANIME
PRODUCED BY: Telecom Animation
Film, 2020–
WRITER: Yoshida Erika
13 episodes

NEXT LEVEL

▶ **The Tower** (where the action takes place) is no simple building. It's an enclosed environment with levels as large as continents (according to **SIU**). The higher the level, the higher the presumed status—but achieving movement between levels means succeeding at **difficult contests**, which may involve **battles** or **intelligence tests**. Those that reach the top level are promised their **greatest desire**.

▶ Of the contestants that climb **the Tower**, **Regulars** are from the residential **Outer Tower** who have been chosen to ascend the **Inner Tower** (where the tests take place). **Regulars** that reach the top become powerful **Rankers**, the administrators of the lower floors. **Bam** is an **Irregular**—one who found his way into the tower without being invited. **Irregulars** bring an element of anarchy to **the Tower**. At the very top of **the Tower** is the mysterious **King Jahad**, vulnerable only to **Irregulars**.

WHERE NEXT?

If you love *Tower of God*, try these South Korean manhwa webtoons:

▶ **SOLO LEVELING** (PICTURED)
Sung Jinwoo is a **novice monster hunter** with an unwell mother to support. After a major defeat, **Jinwoo** awakens with new powers and begins to move up the ranks within a dungeon.

▶ **THE GAMER**
In a similar vein, *The Gamer* features a high school boy who discovers he can perceive the world as a video game. He joins a friend in a secret world called **the Abyss** for all those that share this ability.

STUDIO GHIBLI

World-renowned, international-award-winning Studio Ghibli are beloved by millions for their inventive, heartwarming, animated adventures.

Whether you get a kick from leading giant wolves to stop environmental disasters, following snappily dressed cats into magical realms, or rising above the clouds on a broomstick or biplane, there is a Ghibli film for you!

BREAKDOWN

▶ The Tokyo-based studio was founded by the writer/directors **Miyazaki Hayao** and **Takahata Isao** with producer **Suzuki Toshio** in June 1985. It followed the success of their fantasy movie *Nausicaä of the Valley of the Wind*. The first official movie from the studio was 1986's *Laputa: Castle in the Sky*.

LET'S GET LOST TOGETHER

▶ Opening in 2001, the **Ghibli Museum** in Inokashira Park, Mitaka, Japan, provides a tasteful journey into the worlds of the studios' many movies, including the chance to hop aboard the **Catbus. Miyazaki** wanted the museum to feel like a storybook journey. It has the slogan **"Let's Get Lost Together"** in a place where **"those seeking enjoyment can enjoy, those seeking to ponder can ponder, and those seeking to feel can feel."**

This description can equally be applied to the studio's movies. **Ghibli Park** is a newer attraction based on the movies and opened outside Nagoya, Japan, in 2022. It features life-size reproductions of sets based on *My Neighbor Totoro*, *Kiki's Delivery Service*, and *Howl's Moving Castle*. But there are no theme-park rides if that's what you're looking for!

THE MASCOT

▶ The giant star of 1988's *My Neighbor Totoro* became the logo for the studio from 1991. Characters such as **Totoro**, **No Face**, **Calcifer**, and **Jiji** have led to a hugely successful merchandizing business.

THE CORE
24 official movies
2 TV series

AWARDS
4 Japan Academy Prizes for
Animation of the Year
5 Academy Award nominations
2002 Golden Bear and 2003 Academy
Award win for *Spirited Away*

SNAPSHOT
The word **Ghibli** comes from Miyazaki's love of airplanes. It's an Arabic word for **"hot desert wind"** that was used as the name for an Italian World War II plane. In Japanese, the word is pronounced "Jiburi."

FELINE FASCINATION

▶ **Cats** play a big part in **Ghibli** movies. From **Kiki's** talking cat companion, **Jiji**, in *Kiki's Delivery Service* to **Baron Humbert von Gikkingen** in both *Whisper of the Heart* (1995) and *The Cat Returns* (2002) (PICTURED), to **Bella Yaga's Thomas** in *Earwig and the Witch* (2020). And let's not forget the iconic **Catbus** in *My Neighbor Totoro* (1988). There's always space for a feline face in a **Ghibli** movie. Dogs? Less so.

CGI ARRIVES

▶ **Ghibli** is renowned for **hand-drawn animations**, but some computer animation has snuck in since the 1990s. While **Miyazaki Hayao** remained skeptical of the benefits of computer character design, his son **Gorō** happily adopted the tech for the 2014 TV series *Ronja, the Robber's Daughter* and 2020's *Earwig and the Witch*—the first **Studio Ghibli** feature to go **3DCG** (PICTURED).

Based on a short work by British writer **Diana Wynne Jones** (author of *Howl's Moving Castle,* too), the movie follows a familiar plot for a **Ghibli** movie—a young female trainee witch ends up working in a kitchen. However, the use of 3D imagery disappointed critics. While there's no word on whether or not the studio will experiment with CG in the future, you can expect a return to the hand-drawn look for now.

GHIBLI GROGU

▶ Late 2022, **Disney+** shared a unique crossover between **Studio Ghibli** and **Lucasfilm**—a hand-drawn, short anime *Zen—Grogu and Dust Bunnies*. The sweet three-minute video stars **Grogu**, "Baby Yoda" from *The Mandalorian*, and the dust creatures from *My Neighbor Totoro*. What next? Princess Princess Mononoke vs. Princess Leia?

PRINCESS MONONOKE

▶ The English version of 1997's *Princess Mononoke* was based on a dub screenplay by *The Sandman* and *Coraline* author **Neil Gaiman**. He wrote two versions—one closely based on the Japanese original and one that included feedback from the US studio. His name did not appear on the movie posters, however.

HOW DO YOU LIVE?

▶ Inspired by a 1937 novel by **Yoshino Genzaburō**, the next movie to come from **Ghibli** is *How Do You Live?* described as a two-hour "big fantastical film." The movie is being directed by **Miyazaki Hayao**, and it is expected to be his last. Work began in 2016 and a Japanese release is promised for July 14, 2023.

LIVE TOTORO

▶ Debuting in late 2022, the **stage production** of *My Neighbor Totoro* proved to be the fastest-selling show for **London's Barbican theater**, breaking their record for one-day sales. The story is reimagined for the stage with puppets created by **Basil Twist** and music by **Joe Hisashi** (who provided the original film score). With the show's three-month run sold out, another run will surely be added before long.

MIYAZAKI HAYAO

While not the only creator at Studio Ghibli, Miyazaki Hayao is the company's guiding light.

Miyazaki's imagination is the engine that has powered the studio's output for over 35 years. He's a visionary writer and director with a keen interest in environmental issues and a love of aircraft and cats.

BREAKDOWN

▶ **Miyazaki** launched his career in anime in the 1960s. He was chief animator and scene designer for *The Great Adventure of Horus, Prince of the Sun* in 1968 and the popular action series *Lupin III* and two *Panda! Go, Panda!* shorts in the early 1970s. His first animated feature was a *Lupin III* spin-off named *The Castle of Cagliostro* (PICTURED) in 1979. The movie impressed the publisher of *Animage* magazine, who hired **Miyazaki** to write and draw a manga series that could be adapted into a movie. The result was *Nausicaä of the Valley of the Wind* (manga from 1982–1994, anime 1984), a postapocalyptic fantasy featuring a teen princess protecting a forest of mutant insects from biological attacks.

METHOD

Rather than write a complete screenplay before work begins on a movie, **Miyazaki** works from a rough plan and writes as he designs characters and scenes. Animation work began on the 1992 movie *Porco Rosso* before storyboards had been completed or the ending of the movie had even been scripted!

MIYAZAKI CHECKLIST

Tick these off next time you watch a **Miyazaki** movie:

- ☐ Strong-willed girl
- ☐ Cat
- ☐ Adult who transforms into pig
- ☐ Spirit creature
- ☐ Delicious meal
- ☐ Mountains
- ☐ River
- ☐ Flock of birds
- ☐ European-style buildings
- ☐ House-cleaning
- ☐ Character lying on grass, staring at sky
- ☐ Flying machine

TO RETIRE OR NOT?

▶ **Miyazaki Hayao** has threatened to retire from filmmaking on several occasions—after 1997's *Princess Mononoke*, 2004's *Howl's Moving Castle*, and 2013's *The Wind Rises* (PICTURED) (to concentrate on the Ghibli Museum). As of 2023, he is back at work at age 82 on *How Do You Live?*

THE NEXT MIYAZAKI?

▶ With the **Ghibli** cofounder repeatedly talking retirement, several writer/directors have been touted as his **successor**:

▶ **Mochizuki Tomomi** was the first non-founder to direct a **Studio Ghibli** movie. He directed 1993's *Ocean Waves* but then chose not to remain with the company. He later had success directing anime adaptations of manga hits such as 2010's *House of Five Leaves* and 2016's *Battery*.

▶ **Yonebayashi Hiromasa** was Studio Ghibli's **youngest movie director** when he took on *Arrietty* (2010). The movie was a hit, and **Yonebayashi** followed it with *When Marnie Was There* in 2015, which was nominated for an **Academy Award**. After 18 years with **Ghibli**, **Yonebayashi** helped set up Studio Ponoc. His first movie for the company was 2017's *Mary and the Witch Flower*.

▶ **Hayao's son Miyazaki Gorō** trained as a landscape architect and worked on the **Ghibli Museum** before he got called in to direct *Tales from Earthsea* (2006). Its reception was mixed. He was reluctant to follow in his father's footsteps, but **Gorō** returned to direct 2011's *From Up on Poppy Hill* (PICTURED), and 2020's *Earwig and the Witch* (**Studio Ghibli's** first 3D computer animation).

OURAN HIGH SCHOOL HOST CLUB

(Ōran Kōkō Hosuto Kurabu)

Romantic high school drama *Ouran High School Host Club* is a comedy classic that should have gotten a second series. Set in an elite high school (yes, another!), the series features a forthright female student taking charge of an all-male club and helping them come to terms with their personal problems. It's a show full of character that doesn't take itself too seriously.

BREAKDOWN

▶ When student **Fujioka Haruhi** gains a scholarship to the elite Ouran Academy, she wanders into the abandoned Third Music Room. Here a group of **"the most-handsome male students, with too much time on their hands"** are running their exclusive **Host Club**—entertaining female guests with food and conversation. After accidentally breaking an expensive **Renaissance vase**, Haruhi has to pay for it by doing errands for the club. Due to her short hair, boyish good looks, and natural manner with girls, **Haruhi** is "invited" to become a host and must pretend to be a boy to pay off her debt to the club!

SNAPSHOT

▶ **Hatori Bisco** is the pen name for the creator of *Ouran High School Host Club*. **Bisco's** first manga series was the gothic romance *Millennium Snow*, which ran for 11 years from 2001. Work on the series was interrupted (and never continued) by the huge success of her follow-up, *Ouran High School Host Club*. The protagonist, **Fujioka Haruhi**, was originally meant to be male, but **Bisco** changed the character to a girl who could easily pass as a cute boy. Since 2010, **Bisco** has worked on the sci-fi comedy *Detarame Mōsōryoku Opera*, *Petite Pêche* (2013–2015) and the comedy manga *Behind the Scenes!!* **Bisco** claims inspiration from classic manga such as the supernatural sci-fi *Please Save My Earth* and the basketball manga *Slam Dunk*.

THE CORE
MANGA
PUBLISHED BY: Hakusensha
18 volumes, 2002–2010
WRITER/ARTIST: Hatori Bisco
ANIME
PRODUCED FOR: Bones, 2006
WRITER: Enokido Yōji
26 episodes

THE FLIP SIDE

▶ *Ouran High School Host Club* satirizes Japanese otaku or **"geek"** culture. Obsessive fan groups are often made up of social outsiders with shared interests and many manga/anime stereotypes. For example, the **young boy into cute things**, the **spectacle-wearing aloof type**, and the **narcissist**. The series occasionally breaks the fourth wall (having characters talk to the viewer), **flips conventions**, and plays with **cross-dressing**.

CLASS DIVIDE

▶ The kids of the **Host Club** could easily be portrayed as arrogant when dealing with the less rich student. But in fact, they are mainly polite and curious. The series shows how wealth doesn't automatically bring joy. Each member of the club has their own personal issues and it's **Haruhi** (with her smarts and plain speaking) who helps them open up.

MR PRESIDENT

▶ **Rune Tamaki Rishāru do Gurantēnu**, or **Suō Tamaki** for short, is the flamboyant blond-haired cofounder and president of the **Ouran Host Club**. Half-Japanese and half-French, **Tamaki** is fond of fine clothes and cosplay. As a host, he flatters female guests and behaves with impeccable high-class manners but is mainly clumsy and overly dramatic. **Tamaki** is very drawn to **Haruhi**—especially after recognizing her true gender.

GOING LIVE

▶ While the manga and anime may have wrapped up, *Ouran High School Host Club* found a new life in live action. An 11-episode series based on the manga was broadcast by TBS in Japan in 2011. It starred **Yamamoto Yūsuke** as **Suō Tamaki**, and **Kawaguchi Haruna** as **Fujioka Haruhi**. This was followed by a live-action movie *Ouran High School Host Club* in 2012 and a mobile drama series with the cast the same year.

JUST ONE YEAR

▶ Fans of *Ouran High School Host Club* were disappointed that the anime adaptation never got a second season. The first 26-episode season covered the first eight tankōbon, but not enough of the ongoing manga was completed in time for a second outing. The anime left the relationship between **Haruhi** and club president **Suō Tamaki** unresolved. At least the manga adventure came to a satisfying resolution.

WHERE NEXT?

If you love *Ouran High School Host Club*, try:

▶ **KAGUYA-SAMA: LOVE IS WAR** (PICTURED)
A romantic **high school drama** based around a student council. The bright and down-to-earth female president **Miyuki-san** and wealthy vice president **Kaguya-san** fall in love but are too proud to admit their longing, as it interferes with their ambitions.

▶ **BAKA AND TEST**
Another high school anime that **subverts conventions**. **Yoshii Akiisa** arrives at a new school where students have to battle with magical avatars to earn their grades.

▶ **KISS HIM, NOT ME**
Serinuma Kae is a friendly student obsessed with **yaoi manga**. So obsessed that she imagines the boys at her school as the lovers in her stories rather than admirers of her own.

BOCCHI THE ROCK!

(Bocchi za Rokku!)

Bocchi the Rock! is a rock 'n' roll manga. It follows the fortunes of an introverted lead guitarist as she gains confidence and friends by taking to the stage in a legit live band.

BREAKDOWN

▶ Shy and awkward teenager **Gotō Hitori** dreams of becoming a rock musician. Invited to join **Ijichi Nijika's Kessoku Band**, Hitori has to overcome her anxiety to take to the stage and develop friendships.

MEET THE BAND

The members of the **Kessoku Band** have names based on their real-life counterparts in **J-Rock** band **Asian Kung-Fu Generation**.

▶ **GOTŌ HITORI** is the **shy lead guitarist** who built up a fan base through playing online. But she finds social interaction a serious problem.

▶ **IJICHI NIJIKA** is the **drummer** and **founder**. She's the heart of the band who keeps everyone in time and together. She's great with helping **Hitori** to overcome her nerves, too. Her older sister **Seika** runs the live venue STARRY, where the band rehearse and perform.

▶ **YAMADA RYŌ** is the **bassist**. Aloof and androgynous, **Ryō** attracts other girls without meaning to.

▶ **KITA IKUYO** is the **vocalist** and much more at ease with performing in front of people than **Hitori**. She first joined the band to get closer to **Ryō**.

THE CORE

MANGA
PUBLISHED BY: Honbunsha
5 volumes, 2017–
WRITER/ARTIST: Aki Hamaji

ANIME
PRODUCED BY: CloverWorks, 2022
WRITER: Erika Yoshida
12 episodes

ROCK RIVALS

▶ Other bands that appear in *Bocchi the Rock!* include a psychedelic rock outfit named **Sick Hack** (who share their names with the real band **88Kasyo Junrei**) and a metal band named **Sideros** (who share their last names with **Kinniku Shōjo Tai**).

WHERE NEXT?

If you love *Bocchi the Rock!*, try these other rock band–based anime:

▶ **K-ON!** (PICTURED)
Five teenage girls share friendship and a passion for music when they join their high school **Light Music Club** and prevent it being closed down.

▶ **BECK**
After saving a dog (*Beck*) from bullies, 14-year-old **Tanaka Yukio** discovers the owner, **Ryusuke Minami**, is a **talented guitarist**. Before long, **Yukio** is invited to join **Ryusuke's band** (named after the dog) and finds his purpose in life.

TOP 10
MAGICAL ANIME

Magic thrives in anime. There are fantasy worlds riddled with sorcerers and many, many magical academies with clumsy students mixing up their spells on their way to wizard graduation. Plus, lots of cute animal guardians, too. Here are 10 supernatural sagas worth conjuring in front of your eyeballs.

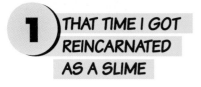

1 THAT TIME I GOT REINCARNATED AS A SLIME

▶ If you had to come back from death in another form, what would you choose? A soaring eagle? A ferocious lion? A great white shark? We're guessing you wouldn't choose a **slime**! That's the fate of poor salaryman **Mikami Satoru**. But this is not a simple slime left behind by a slug, but a slime with **magical powers**—including the ability to absorb the powers of other creatures! As he's reborn in a fantasy realm, the slime befriends a dragon and is renamed **Rimuru Tempest**. He then becomes the leader of a nation. So, now you'd choose a slime, right?

2 PUELLA MAGI MADOKA MAGICA

Cats are the natural partners of **witches**, and *Puella Magi Madoka Magica* is just the first anime in this list to have a feline play an integral part in the plot. In this case, it's a catlike creature named **Kyubey** that tempts two middle school students, **Madoka** and **Sayaka**, by promising them each a wish. The catch is that they must then use magical powers to fight witches. Sounds fun, right? Well, soon after agreeing to the contract, the pair witness an older magical girl's death. **Madoka** and **Sayaka** end up taking opposite sides, with **Madoka** going magical and **Sayaka** becoming a witch. And that cat? He turns out to be an alien sapping magical girls' emotions to save the universe. Oh, and there's more than one timeline, too!

3 LITTLE WITCH ACADEMIA

▶ **"A believing heart is your magic!"** Created by **Yoshinari Yō**, *Little Witch Academia* is kind of a *My Hero Academia* for young witches. It follows **Kagari Atsuko** ("Akko") as she enrolls at Luna Nova Magical Academy, inspired by the witch **Shiny Chariot**. Gifted with **Shiny Chariot's** magical **Shiny Rod**, she helps fellow students revive magic in a world where it's seen as outdated. This coming-of-age adventure has plenty of (magic) charm and comedy. It is as much about building friendships and following your dreams as casting spells.

4 MAGI: THE LABYRINTH OF MAGIC

▶ Based on stories from *One Thousand and One Nights*, *Magi* follows the fortunes of young **Aladdin**, his djinn (genie) **Ugo**, and **Alibaba Saluja**. We see them attempt to capture a mazelike "dungeon" and claim the treasures within. This is just the beginning of the journey for the trio and the many allies they encounter, with **Aladdin** turning out to be the wizard-like Magi of the title. If you enjoy classic fantasy and well-constructed worlds, *The Labyrinth of Magic* is certainly worth losing a few hours in.

5 THE FAMILIAR OF ZERO

▶ Based on the light novels by **Yamaguchi Noboru**, *The Familiar of Zero (Zero no Tsukaima)* tells the story of an aristocratic schoolgirl. Her name is (deep breath!) **Louise Françoise de la Baume le Blanc de la Vallière**. She earns the class nickname **"Louise the Zero"** due to her appalling attempts at wielding magic. Yes, we're in another academy for magic! When the time comes for students to conjure up a protective familiar, **Louise** brings forth a regular teenage boy named **Hiraga Saito**. Huge embarrassment! At first **Louise** treats **Saito** like a lackey, but their relationship develops into much more.

6 THE ANCIENT MAGUS' BRIDE

▶ Rejected by relatives and society, Japanese high school student **Hatori Chise** decides to auction herself and ends up receiving a £5 million (US $5,900,000) bid from a tall humanlike creature with a skull for a head. **Chise** moves in with her new fiancé, **Elias Ainsworth**—his UK home is shared with fairies and other magical beings. It turns out **Elias** is a magus (or powerful magician) who may have once been human but has forgotten his past. **Elias** reveals that **Chise** also has magical abilities and, through her, he hopes to better understand human feelings.

7 CARDCAPTOR SAKURA

▶ Young-girl-meets-cute-animal-guide-and-learns-to-use-magic is a common shōjo trope. Nevertheless, this entry deals a good hand. When 10-year-old **Kinomoto Sakura** accidentally frees a set of magic cards into the world by opening a book, the cute guardian of the cards, **Kero**, appears and tells her she must be magical to have managed it. Given the task of gathering the cards and battling their spirits, young **Sakura** sets out with classmate **Tomoyo** and **Kero** in tow. They take on a range of creatures, testing various powers and dressing in a multitude of outfits.

8 MASHLE: MAGIC AND MUSCLES

▶ You could easily mistake publicity images for *Mashle* with an anime version of Harry Potter. Yes, it's magical academy time again, with **Mash Burnedead** as the student trying to catch up in class in a world where magic is everywhere. He succeeds by using his physical skills to create "Muscle Magic" and works his way up toward his goal of becoming a Divine Visionary.

9 TOILET-BOUND HANAKO-KUN

▶ Up next on this list (for the title if nothing else!) is *Toilet-Bound Hanako-kun*. It's the story of, erm, a high school student who discovers magic. **Yashiro Nene** is fascinated with the supernatural and seeks a legendary spirit that is said to haunt the girls' bathroom at her school and grant wishes. She succeeds in summoning **"Hanako-san of the Toilet"** who turns out to be a boy who Nene must then assist in flushing away evil spirits. (Not literally!)

10 KIKI'S DELIVERY SERVICE

▶ A **Ghibli** classic, *Kiki's Delivery Service* sees a trainee witch take off on her broomstick with a talking cat named **Jiji**. She sets off into the big wide world (which looks like a fantasy European town) and gets hired as a bakery delivery girl. The film includes many **Ghibli** staples—beautifully painted settings, aerobatics, and an optimistic female lead—but most of the movie's magic is in its artistry. *Kiki's Delivery Service* was a huge hit for screenplay writer/director **Miyazaki Hayao** (see page 76), becoming Japan's highest-grossing movie in its year of release.

CASE CLOSED (DETECTIVE CONAN)

When one case closes, another opens. High school detective Conan has been investigating crimes for almost 30 years as one of manga and anime's most enduring characters.

BREAKDOWN

▶ High school student **Jimmy Kudo** was an expert detective. His analytical mind was able to spot clues and patterns that had eluded other investigators. As a teenager, he assisted the police on difficult open cases. But on one investigation, he was ambushed by the criminal **Black Organization** and poisoned. The experimental poison had a surprising effect—it transformed him into a young boy. **Jimmy** took on the identity of **Edogawa Conan** and continued to solve crimes with the help of his childhood friend **Rachel**, her father, Private Eye **Richard Moore**, and members of his school **Junior Detective League**.

SNAPSHOT

▶ Like his hero, **Detective Conan** creator **Aoyama Gōshō** showed talent from a young age. He studied art in Tokyo and won a comic-art contest in his first year, before taking work as a background painter at Tokyo Disneyland. **Aoyama's** manga debut came in 1987 with the story *Chotto Mattete* and was followed by the series *Magic Kaito*—the adventures of phantom thief the **Kaito Kid**. In 1988, **Aoyama** began work on *Yaiba*, which was a popular, long-running saga about a samurai boy. In 1994, **Aoyama** took inspiration from the stories of *Arsène Lupin* and *Sherlock Holmes* to produce the first chapter of *Case Closed* (PICTURED). This has been running as a manga ever since with 270 million copies and counting, and also as an anime with over a thousand episodes. **Aoyama's brothers** (one a **scientist** and one a **doctor**) have been helpful for **Aoyama** as he developed **Conan's** forensic investigations.

THE WORLD'S GREATEST DETECTIVE!

CONAN DOYLE CREATED SHERLOCK HOLMES,

THE CORE

MANGA

PUBLISHED BY: Shogakukan
102 volumes, 1994–
WRITER/ARTIST: Aoyama Gōshō

ANIME

PRODUCED FOR: TMS Entertainment, 1996–
WRITER: Ii'oka Jun'ichi
1,071 episodes
26 movies

DETECTIVE WHO?!

▶ *Case Closed* is known as *Detective Conan* in Japan (actually *Meitantei Konan*). But for legal reasons (possibly because of a fictional barbarian named **Conan**), the series became known as *Case Closed* in translations. Even the main character's true name changed. In English, he is known as **Jimmy Kudo**, but he is **Shinichi Kudo** in Japan, and **Rachel Moore** is **Mōri Ran**. The name of the boy detective, **Edogawa Conan**, is inspired by the Sherlock Holmes author, **Sir Arthur Conan Doyle** and Japanese thriller writer **Edogawa Rampo**.

DARK NEMESIS

▶ **Detective Conan's** long-term aim is to end the criminal reign of the **Black Organization**. Doing so would free him to resume life again as **Jimmy Kudo**. The syndicate is involved in criminal activities with everything from blackmail to assassinations. The agents use drink-based code names. For a long time, the head of the **Black Organization** was kept secret. He only communicated with his agents through text messages. Finally, his identity was revealed as **Karasuma Renya**—a mysterious figure almost 100 years old who supposedly died 40 years ago!

CONAN'S Q

▶ Just like **James Bond**, **Detective Conan** has access to numerous gadgets to help him solve crimes. These are supplied by his neighbor **Dr. Agasa Hiroshi**—one of the only people to know that young **Conan** was once the older **Jimmy Kudo**. Among the gadgets supplied is footwear that boosts **Conan's** strength, **tracking glasses**, a **wristwatch stun gun**, and **braces** that function as **handcuffs**. Possibly the most useful piece of tech is **Conan's voice-altering bow tie**. It enables him to speak using an adult's voice and allows the inept **P.I. Richard Moore** to take the credit for solving cases.

SWITCHING SIDES

▶ Former **Black Organization** agent **Anita Hailey** (Ai Haibara in Japan) was once code named **Sherry** and she was the inventor of the **APTX 4869** chemical that turned **Jimmy** into a boy. After the Organization killed her sister, she drank the same poison and turned into a girl. She now helps **Detective Conan** as a member of his **Junior Detective League**.

LOST LOVE

▶ Being shrunk into the body of a six-year-old means teenage **Jimmy Kudo** can no longer follow up on a potential romance with long-time schoolfriend **Rachel Moore**. Not only is he too young for **Rachel**, but he also wants to protect her from the threat of the **Black Organization**. As **Conan**, he must make excuses for **Jimmy's** "disappearance" and listen to **Rachel** talking longingly of the older boy she has a crush on.

THE CASE CONTINUES

▶ **Aoyama Gōshō** hinted that he had an ending planned for *Detective Conan*, but that was 25 years ago. Crime continues to pay, with an average two tankōbon being published each year, along with new anime episodes and annual movies. The 26th movie, *Detective Conan: Black Iron Submarine*, came out in 2023. *Case Closed* is currently the 15th-longest running anime series, just ahead of *One Piece*.

TO KNOCK THEM OUT WITH THE BALL FROM MY BELT

WHERE NEXT?

If you love *Detective Conan*, try:

▶ **DETECTIVE SCHOOL Q**
With a more varied cast of student detectives than *Case Closed*, *Detective School Q* involves coders, martial artists, and disguise artists working together to clear up whodunits.

▶ **GOSICK** (PICTURED)
Set in Europe in 1924, *Gosick* features Japanese student **Kujō Kazuya** and supersmart **Victorique de Blois** solving crimes together, but **de Blois's** story is as much a mystery that needs to be unraveled.

▶ **GHOST STORIES**
As **Conan's Junior Detective League** gathers to solve crimes, the high school friends in *Ghost Stories* work together to exorcise their town's escaped phantoms.

FRIEREN: BEYOND JOURNEY'S END

(Sōsō no Furīren)

Not your typical fantasy quest tale, *Frieren: Beyond Journey's End* looks at what happens next, with an elven mage trying to understand the brief nature of human lives.

BREAKDOWN

▶ Fifty years after a heroic team (made up of an elf, a dwarf, and two humans) succeeded in their quest to thwart the **Demon King's** plans and bring peace to the world, the long-lived elven mage **Frieren** seeks out her former allies. Soon after the party reunites, the human **Himmel** dies of old age. **Frieren** regrets that she never really got to know him. So she and an apprentice named **Fern** journey to Aureole—the resting place of souls—to say a proper farewell to her comrade.

SNAPSHOT

▶ Writer **Yamada Kanehito** first gained attention for his five-volume manga *Nanashi wa Ittai Dare Deshou? (Who in the World Is the Namelessness?)*. This story of lost memory ran from 2013 to 2015. A follow-up, *Bocchi Hakase to Robot Shoujo no Zetsubou Teki Utopia (The Professor So Lonely He Created a Robot Friend)*, was a post-pandemic story of a scientist living alone with a robot girl. Working with the artist Tsukasa Abe, **Yamada** launched *Frieren: Beyond Journey's End*, in 2020. And this won the New Creator award in the 25th **Tezuka Osamu** awards.

THE CORE

MANGA

PUBLISHED BY: Shogakukan
9 volumes, 2020–
WRITER: Yamada Kanehito
ARTIST: Abe Tsukasa

ANIME

2023–

TIMES PAST

▶ As an elf looking much younger than her thousand years, **Frieren** sees time pass in a different way from her human companions. The 10-year quest she and her fellowship undertook to defeat the **Demon King** seemed a short experience to her. Even though **Frieren** knew **Himmel** for all that time, she thought it a brief acquaintance and felt the need to know more of him. Understanding the nature of humans and their short life spans becomes the new quest for the ancient elf.

THE APPRENTICE

▶ Just as **Frieren** was once the apprentice to the great wizard **Flamme** over a thousand years ago, so is **Fern** to **Frieren**. **Fern** is a human teenager and war orphan from the Southern Lands saved by the priest **Heiter** (another of **Frieren's** deceased human comrades. She is interested in becoming a mage.

Is something the matter?

WHERE NEXT?

If you love *Frieren: Beyond Journey's End*, try:

▶ **RANKING OF KINGS** (PICTURED)
Nicknamed **"The Useless Prince,"** deaf and mute child **Prince Bojji** gains confidence through his friendship with a blobby shadow creature and sets out to become the best king he can be. (See page 144.)

▶ **SOMALI AND THE FOREST SPIRIT**
In a fantasy world where humans are a hunted minority, a **golem** (or watchman of the forest) bonds with a young girl named **Somali** and sets out to find her family.

SAILOR MOON

A shōjo manga that led an anime boom across the world, *Sailor Moon* is a '90s classic beloved by generations. It has now been rebooted and is finding new fans in the 21st century.

When Tokyo middle school student Tsukino Usagi makes friends with a talking black cat named Luna, she is given a magical brooch that turns her into Sailor Moon—a superpowered heroine who can save the world. The pair assemble a team of Sailor Guardians and head on an adventure to find the Silver Crystal. Before long, the Guardians discover they are the reincarnations of protectors from the ancient Moon Kingdom.

LIGHT OF THE MOON

▶ **Takeuchi Naoko** broke into the world of manga at the age of 19 with the title *Love Call*, which won a New Artist Award. After a series of one-shots, she delivered *Maria*, the story of an orphaned girl that ran for several years and *The Cherry Project*, an ice-skating series. In 1991, Takeuchi trialed a space adventure featuring girls in sailor suits, *Codename: Sailor V*. This was well received, so Takeuchi developed it into the series *Sailor Moon*. Takeuchi plotted *Sailor Moon* expecting it to last just 14 chapters, but its popularity meant it was extended to 52 parts. *Sailor Moon* went on to become an international sensation, a franchise earning $13 billion through anime series and movies, video games, dolls, and other merchandise.

SILVER MILLENNIUM

▶ On their first mission against the **Dark Kingdom**, the **Sailor Guardians** discover they had previous lives on the Moon during a period known as the **Silver Millennium**, thousands of years ago. Their **Moon Kingdom** had been destroyed long ago by the Dark Kingdom in a battle over the **Silver Crystal**—but not before the Moon Kingdom's **Queen Serenity** could arrange for her daughter, **Princess Serenity**, **Prince Endymion**, the Guardians, and the feline advisors **Luna** and **Artemis** to be reincarnated on Earth in the future.

MANY NAMES

▶ In Japan, it is **Tsukino Usagi** who transforms into **Sailor Moon**. In early English translations she is **Serena Tsukino** (moving the Japanese family name to the end), but her best friends call her **"Bunny."** In Japanese, her name is a play on the words "tsuki no usagi" which means "rabbit of the moon."

SAILOR SENSHI

The **Sailor Guardians**, or **Sailor Senshi**, gathered by **Luna** include:

▶ **MUZUNO AMI** a shy, supersmart bookworm, who becomes **SAILOR MERCURY**.

▶ **HINO REI** an elegant Shinto princess, who becomes **SAILOR MARS**.

▶ **KINO MAKOTO** a tough, independent student, who becomes **SAILOR JUPITER**.

▶ **AINO MINAKO** a wannabe pop singer, who becomes **SAILOR VENUS**.

▶ They all have unique super-moves. Later stories completed the solar system with further **Sailor Guardians**—**Sailor Pluto**, **Sailor Uranus**, **Sailor Neptune**, and **Sailor Saturn**. And then, there are Guardians from the 30th Century and outside the solar system . . . too many to list here!

THE CORE

MANGA

PUBLISHED BY:
Kodansha, 18 volumes
1991–1997
WRITER/ARTIST:
Takeuchi Naoko

ANIME

PRODUCED FOR: Toei
Animation, 1992–1997
WRITERS: Tomita
Sukehiro, Enokido Yōji,
Yamaguchi Ryōta
200 episodes,
plus 3 TV specials
*Sailor Moon R: The
Movie* 1993
*Sailor Moon S:
The Movie* 1994
*Sailor Moon Super S:
The Movie* 1995

DOOMED LOVE

▶ **The Sailor Guardians** gain a male ally, **Chiba Mamoru** (known as **Darien Shields** in the original English translation). **Mamoru** takes on the identity of **Tuxedo Mask** to aid **Sailor Moon**—though he often finds himself in need of saving.

▶ **Mamoru** is the reincarnation of **Prince Endymion**, who is **Princess Serenity's** true love from the Moon Kingdom. Somehow the pair seemed fated not to get together.

▶ Sadly, **Mamoru** has a tragic background. Both his parents were killed in a traffic accident when he was six. He did not remember events before the crash, but he had recurring dreams about a moon princess. Through the **power of the Silver Crystal**, his memories of being **Prince Endymion** were restored. But, before his love for Serenity could be rekindled, **Mamoru** and the **Sailor Senshi** were killed while trying to protect **Sailor Moon** from the evil **Queen Beryl**. Fear not, death was brief. **Mamoru** and the **Sailor Senshi** were resurrected but lost their memories. It would take another story arc for **Mamoru** to remember, then time travel and several movies for the Moon Kingdom lovers to finally unite.

POWER MOVES

The **Sailor Guardians** fight with many delightfully named super-moves. Here are just a few:

▶ Moon Spiral Heart Attack
▶ Rainbow Double Moon Heartache
▶ Moon Gorgeous Meditation
▶ Silver Moon Crystal Power Therapy Kiss
▶ Starlight Honeymoon Double Therapy Kiss
▶ Hyperspatial Sphere Generate
▶ Mars Flame Sniper
▶ Jupiter Coconut Cyclone
▶ Venus Love and Beauty Shock

THE MIRACLE

▶ **Sailor Moon** is such a popular character in Japan that she has her own store and theme-park attractions. *Pretty Guardian Sailor Moon: The Miracle 4-D* opened for several months in 2018 in Universal Studios in Japan and involved **Sailor Moon** and the Guardians attempting to stop **Youma** stealing visitors' energies. Follow-ups ran in 2019 and 2022.

WISEMAN CHOSE ME TO BE THE LEADER OF OUR DARK WORLD, THE QUEEN OF THE DARK PLANET "NEMESIS"

I AM THE QUEEN OF DARKNESS, BLACK LADY

POSSESSION

▶ While *Sailor Moon* may appear bright and kid-friendly, the show does have its dark moments—including the death of major characters (though the deaths are often swiftly reversed). A recurring theme is brainwashing and possession, pitting friends against friends, and even kids against parents. Later stories include some time-jumping and the introduction of **Chibiusa**, who is the daughter of **Usagi** and **Mamoru** from 1,000 years in the future. She brainwashed **Usagi's** family to make them believe she was a cousin. Returning to the future, and feeling unloved, she is taken over by the **Black Moon Clan's Wiseman** and turned into the **Black Lady** as a portal for dark energy.

21ST-CENTURY REBOOT

▶ 2014 anime *Sailor Moon Crystal* set out to retell the Sailor Moon manga in a more faithful way for the book's 20th anniversary. Three seasons (and 39 episodes) were followed by a two-part film, *Sailor Moon Eternal: The Movie* in 2021. This was followed up with a two-part sequel, *Sailor Moon Cosmos*.

BLEACH

Recruited to guide ghosts to the spirit realm, Kurosaki Ichigo is a Soul Reaper—a hero with supernatural powers, protecting the living and recently deceased from soul-hungry Hollows.

BREAKDOWN

▶ Teenager **Kurosaki Ichigo** has the rare ability to see ghosts. This leads to an encounter with **Kuchiki Rukia**, a **Soul Reaper** who is in town to hunt a **Hollow**—a dangerous lost soul. When **Rukia** is badly injured by the **Hollow** as she protects **Ichigo**, she transfers her power to him. This allows him to continue her mission to send **Hollows** where dead spirits belong. With **Rukia** as his guide, and a team of similarly talented classmates, **Ichigo** learns how to exorcise benign ghosts and battle **Hollows**.

SNAPSHOT

▶ **Kubo Noriaki**, known as **Tite**, was determined to be a mangaka from school age. By 1999, he had fulfilled his dream with his series *Zombiepowder* published in *Weekly Shōnen Jump*. A year later, **Kubo** began developing what would become *Bleach*. He was influenced by the imagery in **Mizuki Shigeru's** *GeGeGe no Kirarō* and the battle sequences in **Kurumada Masami's** *Saint Seiya*. He imagined his **Soul Reapers** dressed in kimonos and armed with guns, but that soon changed to swords. The series was named *"Black"* after the dark kimonos, then *"White,"* and this soon became *"Bleach."* **Kubo** scored a hit, and the manga won a **Shogakukan Manga Award** in 2004. *Bleach's* initial run lasted 15 years and an anime adaptation was launched in 2004. A manga and anime sequel, *Bleach: Thousand-Year Blood War*, followed, along with four movies, and a spin-off by **Kubo** titled *Burn the Witch*.

THE CORE

MANGA
PUBLISHED BY: Shueisha
74 volumes, 2001–2016
WRITER/ARTIST: Kubo Tite

ANIME
PRODUCED FOR: Pierrot, 2004–2012
WRITERS: Sogo Masashi, Kida Tsuyoshi, Shimoyama Kento
366 episodes
Bleach: Thousand-Year Blood War
PRODUCED FOR: Pierrot, 2022–
WRITERS: Taguchi Tomohisa, Hiramatsu Masakl
13 episodes

MOVIES
Bleach: Memories of Nobody 2006
Bleach: The Diamond Dust Rebellion 2007
Bleach: Fade to Black 2008
Bleach: Hell Verse 2010

HOLLOW HORRORS

▶ The ghastly **Hollows** are creatures born from human souls that fail to make the crossing into the afterlife or **Soul Society**, due to a heart full of regret or despair. They are possessed with supernatural powers and crave the souls of both living and dead humans. **Hollows** may be the result of a ghost that has remained in the living world in order to continue a mission, before becoming obsessed with it to a violent degree.

▶ **Hollows** appear in varied forms, but all wear skull-like masks. They may hold a humanlike shape or that of a **lizard** or **demon**. Most are larger and much stronger than humans. To destroy a **Hollow**, a **Soul Reaper** must split its skull in two with a **zanpaku-tō** or a soul-cutting sword. This is said to purify its sins and allow it to progress to the **Soul Society**. If the **Hollow** has committed great sin, it may be dragged into Hell instead.

SOUL SOCIETY

▶ The group responsible for governing lost spirits lives in the **Soul Society**, an afterlife plane. This is the domain of human souls after death until they are reincarnated. Life as a soul is similar to the living world but with slower aging and no hunger. Children are born here, and souls may die.

▶ The balance of **Soul Society** is preserved by the **Soul King**. He resides in the Royal Palace in a separate dimension, protected by the **Royal Guard**. Below the king is a hierarchy of noble houses, judges, and military. Some **Soul Reapers** are allowed to enter the human realm for a limited time to provide konsōs (soul funerals) to lost spirits and to prevent **Hollows** from devouring souls. **Reapers** can only be seen by people sensitive to the supernatural, such as **Kurosaki Ichigo**.

LAWBREAKER

▶ **Kuchiki Rukia** grew up in the **Soul Society** district of **Rukongai** where she showed spiritual powers. Entering the **Shin'ō Academy**, **Rukia** struggled to receive the same privileges and respect given to recruits from noble families. Yet, after decades of training, she was assigned to the Human World and **Karakura Town**, where she was wounded in a battle against a **Hollow** and donated her power to **Kurosaki Ichigo**. But transferring Shinigami powers to humans is forbidden in the **Soul Society**. **Rukia** was arrested and sentenced to death, leading to a showdown between **Kurosaki Ichigo** and the **Reapers** he has been conscripted into.

CUTTING EDGE

▶ **Soul Reapers** are armed with a **zanpaku-tō**, which is a soul-cutting sword that reflects their personality. Through training and finding out the name of the spirit of the sword, a **Reaper** can employ more of the sword's power through different transformations:

▶ **Shikai,** the initial contract between sword and **Soul Reaper**.

▶ **Bankai,** usually achieved after 10 years' training, unleashing the sword's full capacity.

BURN THE WITCH

▶ Set within the same world as *Bleach*, **Kobo Tite's** *Burn the Witch* follows the adventures of **Niihashi Noel** and **Ninny Spangcole**. They're two witches working for the western branch of the **Soul Society** in **Reverse London**— a hidden version of the UK capital, where dragons are monitored and cared for. Named after a 2016 **Radiohead** song, the 2018 one-shot was followed by four more chapters in 2020. A "second season" has been promised. An hour-long anime adaptation was also broadcast in 2020.

WHERE NEXT?

If you love *Bleach*, try:

▶ **SHAMAN KING** (PICTURED)
As a youngster who can talk to spirits, **Asakura Yō** enters a fighting tournament where the winner gets to contact the **Great Spirit** and have a wish granted.

▶ **BLUE EXORCIST**
As with *Bleach*, *Blue Exorcist* involves a group of fighters—led here by the twin sons of Satan—training to hunt malevolent spirits.

▶ **YU YU HAKUSHO**
This '90s hit features a troublesome student who dies saving another kid's life and is given a second chance as a Spirit Detective, solving supernatural mysteries.

SASAKI AND MIYANO

(Kimetsu no Yaiba)

R omantic slice-of-life manga, *Sasaki and Miyano*, tells the story of two male high school students whose relationship becomes much more than friendship.

BREAKDOWN

▶ Handsome first-year student **Yoshikazu Miyano** is a fan of **gay romance manga** and its stories of boys who fall for other boys. He keeps his interest secret, but then he meets **Shūmei Sasaki**. He's an older boy regarded as a troublemaker, who steps in to save a classmate from bullies. Miyano is surprised that Sasaki shares his interest in the genre and their relationship builds.

SNAPSHOT

▶ Mangaka **Harusono Shō** describes her work, *Sasaki and Miyano*, as BL for "Boys' Life" rather than "Boys' Love." She regards it as a story of everyday life as much as a romance. *Sasaki and Miyano* first appeared on the pixiv comic website before being published in nine manga volumes and being translated for anime. **Harusono** has since launched *Butai ni Sake!*, which is the story of an awkward new student named **Asahi Oniwa** who is trying to make friends in a theater club.

THE CORE
MANGA
PUBLISHED BY: Media Factory
9 volumes, 2016–
WRITER/ARTIST: Harusono Shō
ANIME
PRODUCED BY: Studio Deen, 2022–
WRITER: Nakamura Yoshiko
12 episodes, 1 OVA
MOVIE
Sasaki and Miyano: Sotsugyō-hen 2023

HIRANO AND KAGUIRA

▶ Spinning off from *Sasaki and Miyano* from 2019 is *Hirano and Kaguira*, also by **Harusono Shō**. The story follows a blossoming high school male relationship, as **Akira Kaiguira** moves into the school dorms to share a room with "bad boy" **Taiga Hirano**. It is based on a novel **Harusono** published online before the launch of *Sasaki and Miyano*. An anime movie version came out in 2023.

WIDESCREEN

▶ The romance of high school students **Sasaki** and **Miyano** continued on the big screen in early 2023 with the Japanese release of *Sasaki and Miyano: Sotsugyō-hen*. The movie focuses on how the pair's relationship deals with older student **Sasaki** about to graduate.

WHERE NEXT?

If you love *Sasaki and Miyano*, try:

▶ **DOUKYUUSEI** (PICTURED)
When top-scoring student **Sajou Rihito** needs help for a chorus festival, school guitarist **Kusakabe Hikaru** offers to help. The pair begin to bond through the songs they share.

▶ **BUTAI NI SAKE!**
Same writer, two boys, another school. *Butai ni Sake!* features a shy student overcoming his struggles with socializing by joining a theater club and making his stage debut.

TOP 10
ULTRA UPGRADES

From super-fan to superhero, disciple to ninja, mecha to galaxy-spanning mega-being—giving characters a major muscle makeover is all part of anime. Here are 10 phenomenal power-ups that pump up a hero's power to off-the-scale levels.

1 DRAGON BALL
SUPER SAIYAN

▶ Two, Three, God, Blue, in whatever combination, **Super Saiyan** is the most iconic anime transformation. Any **Saiyan** with enough **S-Cells** can become a once-legendary **Super Saiyan**, through rage or sadness. It provides the wielder with at least 10 times their base power output, plus quite spectacular spiky hair! Of the most recent upgrades for **Goku**, **Perfect Ultra Instinct** is the most impressive. It gives **Goku** another level of speed and strength (along with gray hair, a shredded shirt, and a risk of exploding).

FIRST SEEN: *Dragon Ball* manga Chapter 317, anime episode 95 "Transformed at Last."

2 NARUTO SHIPPŪDEN

NINE TAILS CHAKRA MODE

▶ The **Nine-Tailed Demon Fox** contained in the body of ninja **Uzumaki Naruto** since childhood is the source of his powers. Taking advantage of the demon's chakra boosts **Naruto's** strength, speed, durability, and stamina to next-level awesomeness! It also lights him up like a candle. This significant power-up gives **Naruto** the ability to whack the **White Zetsu Army** with one kick and brush off lava attacks from **Roshi**. Initially, **Naruto** risks his own **chakra**—and life—while using that of **"Nine Tails"** (Kurama). Once the demon begins cooperating, **Naruto** can use the mode without limitations.

FIRST SEEN: Naruto manga Chapter 499 "A New Seal!!," Naruto: Shippūden anime episode 247 "Target: Nine-Tails."

3 GURREN LAGANN

SPIRAL POWER

▶ When metal fists are not enough, how about the ability to toss galaxies around like Frisbees? That's the power level reached by the mecha *Gurren Lagann* using the combined **Spiral Power of Team Gurren**. **Tengen Toppa** means "Heaven-piercing" and size-wise, it propels the mecha to 100,000,000,000,000,000,000,000,000 his usual volume, as a higher-dimensional being several light-years across and able to wield galaxy-size rifles to take down **Antispiral**.

FIRST SEEN: Gurren Lagann anime episode 27 "The Lights in the Sky Are Stars."

4 HUNTER X HUNTER

LIMITATION TRANSFORMATION

▶ When **Hunter Gon Freecss** makes a **Nen contract** to access all the power he would ever have in his life, he's transformed from a boy to an adult to cope with this massive boost. **Gon's** new attributes include **incredible strength** and **superfast speed** that makes him appear to vanish. His upgrade may bring him up to **Chimera Ant King Meruem** levels—not that we get to see that face-off.

FIRST SEEN: Hunter x Hunter anime episode 131 "Anger X and X Light."

5 JOJO'S BIZARRE ADVENTURE
ULTIMATE LIFE-FORM

▶ When **Kars** (leader of the **Pillar Men**) combines the **Stone Mask** and **Red Stone of Aja**, he can survive the sun's lethal rays and transform into his ultimate form—a being with godlike powers. And how does he demonstrate his new abilities? He turns his hand into a squirrel. OK, this is not your typical backyard squirrel, but a flesh-eating one that can punch through metal. **Kars** now has control over his own DNA and can detach parts of his body and have them mimic any life-form. That includes sprouting wings!

FIRST SEEN: *JoJo's Bizarre Adventure*, manga Chapter 109 "Kars the Ultimate Being Is Born, Part 1," anime episode 25 "The Birth of a Superbeing."

6 MY HERO ACADEMIA
ONE FOR ALL

▶ Nerdy schoolkid **Izuku** is the only one in his class without a **Quirk**. But what he lacks in powers, he holds in courage. **Japan's number-one superhero, All Might**, recognizes this and grants him his own **Quirk, One for All**. It isn't one that comes overnight. **Izuku** has to train for years with help from **Endeavor**—preparing his body so it can cope with the many **Quirks** unlocked by **One for All**. After taking the name **Deku**, he is well on his way to reaching the power levels of his first mentor.

FIRST SEEN: *My Hero Academia* manga Chapter 1 "Izuku Midoriya: Origin," anime episode 2 "What It Takes to be a Hero."

7 FAIRY TAIL
DRAGON FORCE

▶ This power-up sees dragon slayers gain their **"true form"** as **virtual dragons**. For **Natsu Dragneel**, chomping on pure magic crystals of **Etherion** boosts his powers over fire, plus speed, strength, and durability. This temporary boost has an unwelcome side effect of wretched stomach pains and scaly skin. **Natsu** later manages to obtain the **Dragon Force** without an unpleasant meal, the first-known **First Generation Dragon Slayer** to do so.

FIRST SEEN: *Fairy Tail* manga Chapter 98 "Dragon Force," anime episode 40 "Titania Falls."

8 BLEACH
BANKAI

▶ The **Shinigami** have two powered-up modes—**Shikai** and **Bankai** (First and Final Release). The first involves learning the name of and communicating with the **zanpaku-tō** spirit in their soul-cutter sword; the second draws the spirit into the corporeal world and usually requires 10 years of training. Few **Soul Reapers** reach this high technique. **Kurosaki Ichigo** and **Urahara Kisuke** took a risky shortcut by using a device to materialize a **zanpaku-tō** spirit by force within three days.

FIRST SEEN: *Bleach* manga Chapter 127, "Beginning of the Death of Tomorrow," anime episode 45 "Overcome your Limits."

9 DIGIMON
MEGA FORM

▶ **Digimons** have several forms they can evolve into—their In-Training form, **Rookie**, **Champion**, **Ultimate**, then the short-lived **Mega Form**. Abilities differ between **Digimon** but, for **Wargreymon** (Agumon's Mega Form), this lets him use **Gaia Force** to create an exploding star with his hands and send it hurtling toward his foes. That is some extreme form of catch!

FIRST SEEN: *Digimon Zero Two* anime episode 39 "Dramon Power."

10 ONE PIECE
GEAR CHANGE

▶ **Monkey D. Luffy's** elastic abilities gifted to him by the **Devil Fruit** might at first seem a feeble superpower, but his gear changes stretch it to impressive limits. **Luffy** works out how to increase his blood flow, pump up his muscles, and whip his rubbery limbs at high speed for **Gear Second**. For **Gears 3 and 4**, **Luffy** inflates parts of his body to form giant fists and mega-muscles—he can even compress and expand his body to propel it through the air. **Gear 5** is on a whole other level, though, making use of the **Devil Fruit's** innate powers, allowing **Luffy** to turn things around him into rubber.

FIRST SEEN: *One Piece* manga Chapter 387 "Gear," anime Chapter 272 "Luffy is in Sight! Gather at the Courthouse Plaza."

TEZUKA OSAMU

Thought of as "the father of manga," Tezuka Osamu was a pioneer and major inspiration for aspiring mangaka. He created one of the medium's most famous and enduring characters, **Astro Boy**.

BIRTH OF A GENIUS

▶ Over his 40-year career **Tezuka Osamu** wrote and drew an astonishing **150,000 pages of manga** and worked on about **60 animated features**. His prolific and influential career laid the groundwork for the industry.

▶ **Tezuka** was born in 1928 and was a keen artist from childhood. He grew up a huge fan of movies, especially **Disney** animations, and comics, including many imported from the United States. The young **Tezuka** had to put aside his ambitions through World War II. He saw the devastation caused by air raids on his home in Osaka. The horrors of the war compelled him to promote peace and justice through his comic work.

▶ Postwar, there were few opportunities for Japanese manga artists, but the 19-year-old **Tezuka** managed to find work illustrating *Shin-Takarajima (New Treasure Island)*. It was written by **Sakai Shichima** and loosely based on **Robert Louis Stevenson's** 19th-century *Treasure Island*. **Tezuka** roughed out 250 pages for the book, but only 60 were included when the title was published in 1947. Despite the severe editing, the book was a huge hit, selling **400,000 copies** to a manga-starved public.

ROARING SUCCESS

▶ **Tezuka** was allowed more pages for his next projects, a trilogy of sci-fi epics, *Lost World* (1948), *Metropolis* (1949), and *Next World* (1951). These were followed by a "roaring" success, *Kimba the White Lion*, which was serialized from 1950 to 1954. Published as *Jungle Emperor* in Japan, the manga tells the story of a young lion born aboard a ship bound for a zoo. The lion then escapes and grows up to help Africa's wild animals live in harmony with one another and humans.

THE CORE

KEY MANGA

New Treasure Island 1947
Metropolis 1949
Kimba the White Lion 1950–1954
Astro Boy 1952–1968
Princess Knight 1953–1968
Phoenix 1954–1988
Dororo 1967–1968
Buddha 1972–1983
Black Jack 1973–1983
Message to Adolf 1983–1985

KEY ANIME

Tales of a Street Corner 1962
Astro Boy 1963–1966
The Amazing 3 1965–1966
Kimba the White Lion 1965–1967
Princess Knight 1967–1968
Dororo 1969
A Thousand and One Nights 1969
Marvelous Melmo 1971–1972
Little Wansa 1971–1972
Triton of the Sea 1972
Jetter Mars 1977
Astro Boy 1980
Phoenix 2772 1980
Jumping 1984
Self Portrait 1988

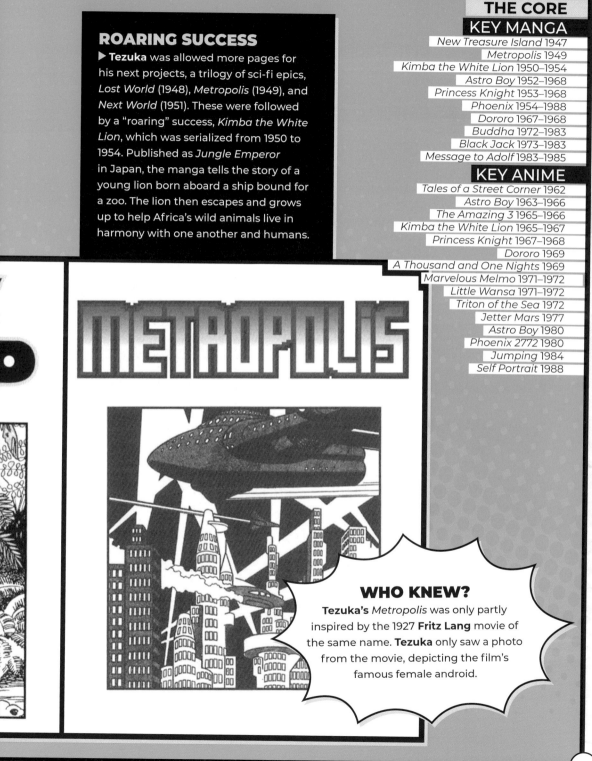

WHO KNEW?

Tezuka's *Metropolis* was only partly inspired by the 1927 **Fritz Lang** movie of the same name. **Tezuka** only saw a photo from the movie, depicting the film's famous female android.

MIGHTY ATOM

▶ In 1951, **Tezuka** published the short manga series *Ambassador Atom*. It included the first appearance of the character who would be known as *Astro Boy* (see page 112). Adapted for his own series from 1952, **Astro Boy** became a phenomenon, with an initial run that lasted until 1968 and an anime series that sold worldwide.

▶ In 1953, **Tezuka** introduced a manga aimed at the shōjo market, *Princess Knight (Ribon no Kishi)* (PICTURED). This is a fantasy drama featuring a girl who pretends to be a male prince to protect the throne of Silverland. A year later, **Tezuka** began a project he considered his life's work, *Phoenix (Hi no Tori)*. He returned to the series on and off over the next decades, but this **time-jumping saga** of immortality would never reach its conclusion as **Tezuka** would not live to complete it.

THE PRINCE IS HERE!

MUSHI PRODUCTION

▶ The success—and volume—of **Tezuka's** manga work helped him raise enough money to launch his own animation company, **Mushi Production**. In 1963, it brought *Astro Boy* to anime life in black-and-white, followed by *Kimba* in 1965—the first Japanese animation produced in full color. Despite success with these early series, **Mushi Production** didn't make enough money, so production ended in 1973.

▶ Returning to manga, **Tezuka** began to adopt a more mature drawing style for an adult audience. He launched the magazine *COM* and the dark-fantasy series *Dororo* (PICTURED) in 1967. He dealt with heavy issues such as the rise of the Nazis with 1983's *Message to Adolf*. Even tackling dark or serious subjects, **Tezuka's** artwork kept its charm and cinematic dynamism.

▶ **Tezuka** died of stomach cancer in 1989. His dying words as his drawing tools were taken away were reported to be, **"Please, please let me continue to work . . ."** A museum celebrating his life and work, named the **Takarazuka City Tezuka Osamu Memorial Hall**, opened in 1994.

SHORT CUTS

▶ **Tezuka's** experimental side was expressed in a series of short animations he produced over the years—many of which won international awards. *Tales of the Street Corner* (1962) is a wordless anime featuring a girl trying to retrieve a lost toy bear. *Pictures of an Exhibition* (1966) is a series of anime set to the music of the Russian composer, **Modest Mussorgsky**. **Tezuka** also directed animated movies for adults, including *A Thousand and One Nights* (1969) and *Cleopatra* (1970).

CAST OF CHARACTERS

▶ The secondary characters in **Tezuka's** books would often make cameo appearances in other titles, under different names. **Tezuka** treated his cast like a "star system" of actors, with personalities taking on other roles. For example, **Astro Boy's** schoolmaster **Mustachio (Ban Shunsaku)** could reappear as a detective. His "father" **Dr. Ochanomizu** turned up as authority figures in *Black Jack*. Among **Tezuka's** cast is a version of himself in his signature beret. Sometimes he introduces his stories, and other times he plays a key character, as in *The Vampires* (1966) or a school classmate of the doctor *Black Jack* (1973).

SHIPS GO MISSING.

MEDICINE MAN

▶ Despite his early creative workload, **Tezuka** attended medical school and qualified as a doctor of Western medicine. He gave up this career for his first love of manga and anime, but his knowledge of medicine worked its way into one of his later stories. *Black Jack* tells the tale of a traveling doctor, **Hazama Kurō**, whose hair and face are discolored due to an explosion during his childhood that also killed his mother. While charging outrageous surgery fees to those that can afford it, the dashing doctor donates most of his money to charity.

ASTRO BOY
(Tetsuwan-Atomu)

Astro Boy is one of the most famous and enduring Japanese characters.

He's a childlike robot with human emotions, a kind heart, and great mechanical powers. Tezuka Osamu's android creation led a manga and anime revolution and remains an international icon.

BREAKDOWN

▶ In a future where robots live with humans, **Tobio** (the son of Ministry of Science director **Dr. Tenma Umataro**) is killed in a tragic vehicle accident. The doctor decides to build a robotic boy to replace him. The robot has human emotions, but **Tenma** rejects him—he realizes the robot cannot take his son's place. The robot (now named **Astro**) is then discovered performing in a circus by the new Ministry of Science director **Professor Ochanomizu Hiroshi** who adopts him. With a kind new mentor, **Astro Boy** begins attending elementary school. The professor upgrades him with extraordinary robot powers to defend Earth against alien attack, dangerous robots, or villains.

SNAPSHOT

▶ **Tezuka Osamu** (see page 108) introduced his robotic boy character in a short story, "Ambassador Atom" for *Shōnen* boys' magazine in April 1951, while he was still studying to be a doctor. The character proved popular, and **Tezuka** gave him human emotions. He also made him the star of a new manga, *Tetsuwan-Atomu*, or *Mighty Atom*. This was translated as *Astro Boy* in English-speaking countries.

▶ The series ran from 1952 to 1968 and was adapted by **Tezuka's** own **Mushi Production** as an animated TV series. It is considered the first popular show that could truly be described as anime.

POWERS

Professor Ochanomizu improved on **Dr. Tenma's** design of **Astro Boy**, giving him a series of mechanical powers that turned the robot into a superhero. These include:

▶ Rocket boots
▶ 100,000 horsepower engine
▶ Rear-end blasters
▶ Amplified hearing
▶ Fluency in over 60 languages
▶ Searchlight eyes

Ochanomizu also built him a robotic family, including parents, sister **Uran**, and brother **Cobalt**.

THE CORE
MANGA
PUBLISHED BY: Kobunsha, 23 volumes
WRITER/ARTIST: Tezuka Osamu
1952–1968
ANIME
PRODUCED BY: Mushi Production, 1963–1966
WRITER: Tomino Yoshiyuki
193 episodes
PRODUCED BY: Tezuka Productions, 1980–1981
WRITER: Tezuka Osamu and others
52 episodes
PRODUCED BY: Tezuka Productions, 2003–2004
WRITER: Marc Handler
50 episodes
MOVIE
Mighty Atom: The Brave in Space 1964
WRITERS: Rintaro, Suzuki Yoshitake, Yamamoto Eiichi

INTERNATIONAL ORDERS

▶ *Astro Boy* debuted on Japanese TV on New Year's Day in 1963. It would be the first Japanese animation dubbed into English for an American audience, for broadcast that year. The US order for 52 episodes provided the funds for **Mushi Production** to continue, but it directed the content of the stories. The US NBC network requested that the cartoons were not set in Japan, and all stories had to be wrapped up in one episode.

▶ The huge order for episodes from the United States meant more stories had to be written than the manga could supply, so **Tezuka** created new adventures for **Astro Boy** that only appear in the anime.

▶ Following its debut in Japan and the United States, *Astro Boy* was broadcast in the UK, France, Germany, Australia, Taiwan, Hong Kong, Thailand, and the Philippines.

REBOOTS AND REVISIONS

▶ An enduring character, *Astro Boy* has been adapted for three anime series. The first two were overseen by creator **Tezuka Osamu's Mushi Pro** and **Tezuka Productions**. The 1980 version was a color remake of the original black-and-white 1963 series. A later version was produced in 2003 (after the death of **Tezuka**) for the 40th anniversary of the anime. It kept the retro-futuristic look of the original, but this newer series featured more serious themes and conflicts in its story lines. A US CGI *Astro Boy* movie was released in 2009 with **Freddie Highmore** as the voice of **Astro Boy** in the English dub.

MIGHTY MASCOT

In 1966, **Astro Boy** was chosen as the **mascot for the Japanese professional baseball team**, Sankei Atoms. He was also named as Japan's envoy for overseas safety in 2007.

THE OTHER ASTRO

▶ **Tezuka** planned an *Astro Boy* anime color reboot in 1977 for **Toei Animation**. But they weren't able to get the copyright for his character, so **Tezuka** developed a new robot hero named **Jetter Mars**. While the character's futuristic setting (2015!) and some of his story lines are similar to *Astro Boy*, the series did not take off, and the show ended after 27 episodes. Once **Tezuka** regained the rights to *Astro Boy*, he returned to his original plan. *Jetter Mars* does have charm, though, and has since become a cult favorite.

CAUGHT IN BETWEEN

▶ In the manga series, **Astro Boy** finds himself caught between two worlds. While he is able to make friends at school, he is not fully accepted or trusted by humans. The robot community also treats him with suspicion.

SELF-SACRIFICE

▶ **Astro Boy** is often damaged from his battles and in need of repair—he even sacrifices himself to save humanity. In the **final episode** from the original anime series, he rockets into the Sun to prevent the planet overheating.

I WANT YOU TO WRITE A MANGA WITH ME.

BAKUMAN

Bakuman is a manga about manga. It follows two creators as they struggle to succeed in the world of Japanese comics. A drama, love story, and slice-of-life that often uses manga titles that exist in the real world. Not only was *Bakuman* a bestseller, but it was also the first manga to be released online in multiple languages before Japanese print copies went on sale. It's a love song to manga and those who create it.

BREAKDOWN

▶ A story of friendship, creativity, and love, *Bakuman* follows artist **Mashiro Moritaka** and writer **Takagi Akito**, as they progress from beginners to professionals in the manga industry. Not only is it about the love of their art, but **Mashiro's** love for **Azuki Miho**—his childhood sweetheart who promises to marry him when they both achieve their dreams. Using the pen name of **Ashirogi Muto**, **Takagi** and **Mashiro** begin creating manga and must face all the struggles, hopes, and fears that come with creativity.

SNAPSHOT

▶ **Ōba Tsugumi** and **Obata Takeshi** worked together on the best-selling manga *Death Note* (PICTURED) before creating *Bakuman*. **Ōba Tsugumi** is a pen name—the writer's real name is a mystery. According to the profile from *Death Note*, he collects teacups. More is known of artist **Obata Takeshi**. Born in 1969 in Niigata, **Obata** was mentored under **Niwano Makoto** before writing and drawing *Cyborg Jii-chan G* in 1989 and *Hikaru no Go* in 1998.

THE CORE

MANGA
PUBLISHED BY: Shueisha
20 volumes, 2008–2012
WRITER: Ōba Tsugumi
ARTIST: Obata Takeshi

ANIME
PRODUCED FOR: J.C.Staff, 2010
WRITER: Yoshida Reiko
75 episodes

NOVEL
PCP—Perfect Crime Party
WRITER: Hatsuno Sei
Published by: Sheisha, 2015

MOVIE
Bakuman 2015
DIRECTED BY: One Hitoshi

FROM THE ONE NOTEBOOK LOST IN THE HUMAN WORLD BY THIS SHINIGAMI...

WHAT'S IN A NAME?

▶ According to **Obata Takeshi**, the title of the series *Bakuman* is a combination of several ideas. "Bakuhatsu" means "explosion," "bakuichi" means "gamble," and "baku" is an animal that eats dreams. They serve to give the idea of what it means to be a creator.

CREATIVE FORCES

▶ MASHIRO MORITAKA

Mashiro is also called **Saikon** by his friends and is the main hero of *Bakuman*. He's extremely talented and driven. He can also be **competitive**—especially when it comes to his rival **Niizuma**. He worshipped his uncle, **Mashiro Nobuhiro**, a manga artist who worked himself to death.

▶ TAKAGI AKITO

Takagi is the other half of the **Ashirogi Muto** pen name and friend of **Mashiro**. **Akito** is a talented writer and, like his friend, works hard to be the best he can. While thoughtful, he can have a temper and doesn't take bad reviews well.

▶ AZUKI MIHO

A **shy** but **ambitious** schoolgirl, **Miho** wanted to become a successful voice actress. She fell in love with **Mashiro** when she was young but believed that they should only get married when they had both succeeded in achieving their dreams— she didn't want their love distracting them from their goals.

▶ MIYOSHI KAYA

At school, **Kaya** was a big supporter of **Takagi** and **Mashiro's** desire to become **mangaka**, and she often helped them with their work. It turns out that she also has feelings for **Takagi**. She's a black belt in **karate**, and she took up **kickboxing**, too.

STAND UP

▶ While *Bakuman* has ended, artist **Obata Takeshi** has been working on a new strip with writer **Asakura Akinari**. *Show-ha Shoten!* is about two high school students trying to become comedians.

MANGA IN MANGA

▶ "Ashirogi Muto" creates several manga series within *Bakuman*. Their first main series is *Detective Trap* (PICTURED). Published in *Weekly Shōnen Jump* (at least in the *Bakuman* world), *Detective Trap* is about a detective who cons criminals intro revealing their plans. The team's next strip is *Run, Daihajsu Tanto!* It's a comedy strip about a young kid who has crazy adventures, thanks to machines his mad inventor grandfather makes. *PCP* is the first **Ashirogi** strip to gain real popularity. *Perfect Crime Party (PCP)* was about a group of school friends who would try to perform the perfect crimes. After this strip, they created their most successful work, *Reversi*. It follows a man who gains the power to transmit his thoughts and ideas to other people, just by touching them. He soon finds himself trying to change the world.

WHERE NEXT?

If you enjoyed *Bakuman*, try:

▶ **GENSHIKEN** (PICTURED)
A teenager lacking in confidence joins his college's club for the **Study of Modern Visual Culture** (also known as **Genshiken**), and he slowly starts to come out of his shell and realize his love for fantasy and manga.

▶ **BECK: MONGOLIAN CHOP SQUAD**
Like *Bakuman*, *Beck* deals with an artist trying to achieve his dreams with life-changing results. In this case it's a young musician who realizes it's time to make a stand—both onstage and in his life.

▶ **TIME PARADOX GHOSTWRITER**
While it also deals with the creation of manga, this series comes with a sci-fi twist as the creator starts to find copies of *Weekly Shōnen Jump* from 10 years in the future.

LAID-BACK CAMP
(Yuru Camp)

Laid-Back Camp is a charming tale of friendship between high schoolers who bond through their mutual love of camping. It is one of the most popular Iyashikei-style stories—Iyashikei are slice-of life tales often dealing with everyday events and friendships in a warmhearted style. *Laid Back Camp* isn't just about friendship, though—it's a relaxing treat, filled with the joys of nature and the great outdoors.

BREAKDOWN

▶ **Shima Rin** loves solo camping. But when she helps fellow high schooler **Kagamihara Nadeshiko,** the two become friends and are soon joined by others who love the great outdoors. Together they join the **Outdoor Activities** club at their high school.

SNAPSHOT

▶ **Afro** lives in Kōfu, the capital city of Yamanashi Prefecture, Japan. His first manga work was *Monday Flying Orange*, which ran for two volumes. He also created *Parallel Worlds Do Not Remain Parallel Forever*, *Shirokuma to Fumeikyoku*, and *Mono*. *Laid-Back Camp* started in 2015 and has proved to be a huge success. It was originally serialized in *Manga Time Kirara Forward* before moving to *Comic Fuz* in 2019. *Laid-Back Camp* has also been turned into a popular anime, live-action movie, and several video games. Afro recently created a crossover between his two main hits, *Laid-Back Camp* and *Mono*.

THE CORE

MANGA
PUBLISHED BY: Houbunsha
14 volumes, 2015–
WRITER/ARTIST: Afro

ANIME
PRODUCED BY: Crunchyroll
WRITER: Tanaka Jin
25 episodes
Anime movie 2022

LIVE ACTION
PRODUCED BY: TV Tokyo
2020–2021
24 episodes

HAPPY CAMPERS

While **Shima Rin** enjoys camping alone, she soon makes new friends . . .

▶ **KAGAMIHARA NADESHIKO** A **happy**, **upbeat** girl who **loves eating** and often **forgets** things. She befriends **Rin** and becomes a member of the Outdoor Activities club. Ashe shares the same birthday as her friend **Inuyama Aoi.**

▶ **OGAKI CHIAKA** The **Outdoor Activities club leader**. Her birthday is August 31.

▶ **SAITŌ ENA** Rin's **classmate**, who always appears happy. She also owns a cute dog called **Chikuwa**.

▶ **INUYAMA AOI** Chiaka's close friend and co-president of the Outdoor Activities club. She is from Inuyama.

▶ **TOBA MINAMI** The Outdoor Activities club advisor and a teacher at **Rin's** school.

WHERE NEXT?

If you love *Laid-Back Camp*, try:

▶ **ARIA**
Young **Aria** only wants to be a gondolier—on Mars. The series follows **Aria's** attempts to achieve her dream in her beautiful and futuristic world.

▶ **SENRYU GIRL**
This hit show is a wonderful story about a girl, **Nanako**, who can only communicate using short poems.

▶ **NON NON BIYORI** (PICTURED)
Follows a group of girls living in the lovely village of Asahigaoka, showing their daily lives in their picturesque, rural home.

TOP 10

WORLD-BUILDING SERIES

World building is the act of creating a believable reality for a story. Some stories—like The Lord of the Rings—have complex histories, maps, and even languages. Others—like Harry Potter—build the reality of the hero's world as the story progresses. Manga and anime are filled with spectacular examples of world building. The following represent some of the best, from magical and mysterious realms to scary and dangerous futures.

1 THE SEVEN DEADLY SINS

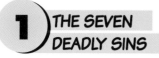

▶ A magical adventure set in a fully reimagined world that has more than a passing resemblance to **medieval Europe**. Part of the show's success is the fully realized background to the saga. It follows a young girl, **Elizabeth**, seeking out legendary heroes when the **kingdom of Britannia** is taken over by vicious **Holy Knights**. With its roots firmly in European and Arthurian legend, it's a fun, epic saga in a rich and magical world, complete with knights, monsters, and all sorts of strange creatures—including the terrifying members of the **Demon Clan**.

2 BLACK CLOVER

▶ The magical world of *Black Clover* is set in a reality where everyone has access to magical abilities (apart from the hero, **Asta**). From the grimoire selection ceremonies of would-be **mages** to the rankings of the **Magic Knight order**, *Black Clover* excels at creating a society where sorcery is a very real part of everyday life. It's a background that only gets more enthralling and more complex as we follow **Asta** and **Yuno** on their attempt to become the **Wizard King**—confronting some deadly and demonic entities along the way. With magic and anti-magic, strange monsters, and a rich history—not to mention a good dash of humor—*Black Clover* is one of the best realized fantasy realms in manga.

3 ARIA

▶ Not all world building results in fantastical and dangerous worlds. *Aria* is a slice-of-life manga set on **Mars** in the 24th century. The planet has been renamed **Aqua**, and the hero, **Akari**, is training to be a gondolier with the **Aria gondoliers**. With so many manga and fantasy worlds filled with demons and monsters, it makes a real change to travel to a fully realized world full of peace and hope. The stories move at a nice calm pace, allowing the reader to take in the beautiful environments of Neo-Venezia (**Akari's** Venice-like new home) and the terraformed Mars.

4 AKIRA

▶ Few manga have been as popular or as influential as *Akira*. The futuristic, cyberpunk epic was one of the first anime to make a huge impression in the West—the manga even got a **Marvel** reprint as part of their **Epic line**. The story saw gang leader **Kaneda** try to rescue his friend from a corrupt government facility. Set in Neo Tokyo after the city was devastated by a nuclear bomb in 1988, the story is a mix of conspiracies, corruption, and secret experiments. It's all about edge-of-your-seat action and high-octane drama in a cyberpunk future—one that continues to influence creators of all genres.

5 MADE IN ABYSS

▶ Manga has some incredibly inventive worlds. One of the stranger ones is found in *Made in Abyss*. The story is set in a world where a vast abyss appeared filled with mystical objects that can be collected by those brave (or foolish) enough to venture into its depths. The area around the Abyss is strange with increasingly dangerous levels, plus the curious sights and creatures are all wonderfully thought out. The "Delvers" (those people who venture into the Abyss) include the main hero, **Riko**. She not only wants to follow in her mother's footsteps but she is also determined to solve the mystery of her disappearance.

6 NAUSICAÄ OF THE VALLEY OF THE WIND

▶ Set a thousand years after the world was almost destroyed in the **Seven Days of Fire**, *Nausicaä of the Valley of the Wind* is one of the best glimpses of a strange, post-apocalyptic world. It features a princess named **Nausicaä** as she tries to restore the bond between humanity and the Earth. It's a beautifully realized world where humans live in small cities and travel by airships while the jungles are filled with strange insects and other creatures. Like the best realized worlds, it is both different and relatable at the same time, and the film carries an important environmental message.

7 DR. STONE

▶ *Dr. Stone* takes world building to a new level as the hero, **Senku**, and his allies are literally rebuilding civilization from scratch. Set 3,500 years after everyone in the world was turned to stone, **Senku** uses science to slowly bring the world back to life—and uncover what caused the original petrification. Built on a brilliantly bizarre idea, the series is a love song to science, with ace characters and a cool sense of humor. The show begins with a small cast but soon develops more characters as Senku invents ways to reverse the petrifaction process . . . only to learn that some of his friends oppose his ideas.

SPIRITED AWAY

▶ Hailed as one of the **greatest anime movies of all time**, *Spirited Away* was directed by **Miyazaki Hayao** (page 76). The story follows 10-year-old **Ogino Chihiro** as she tries to rescue her parents after they visit a strange mystical realm. The dreamlike quality of the film enhances the unusual creatures (many based on Japanese myths) that **Chihiro** encounters on her fantastical quest. While strange and unknown, this world is also nightmarishly real. It is world building, but not in a fully realized *Black Clover* way. Instead it creates a surreal bubble that serves to enhance **Chihiro's** journey.

 **MAGI: THE LABYRINTH OF MAGIC**

▶ Often world building uses well-known myths as the core of the story. One of the best examples of this is *Magi: The Labyrinth of Magic*. The series uses the *Arabian Nights (One Thousand and One Nights)* as its inspiration, bringing creatures such as **djinn** into manga. The story involves dungeons, magi (basically powerful magicians), and adventurers—all set in a world where magic is very much part of life. The action is set 14 years after thousands of people vanished into a strange new structure that appeared and follows two friends **Alibaba Saluja** and **Aladdin**.

10 **ATTACK ON TITAN**

▶ Soma manga take their time to build up the setting while others throw the reader straight into the action. *Attack on Titan* might be one of the more violent manga, but it is also a classic example of successful world building. The new world order is established from the start. Giants have appeared—the **Titans**—and they've started to feast on humanity. The human survivors now live in a vast walled city and have established special squads to protect their new homes from their ravenous enemies. At the start of the series, the survivors have been in their new walled city for over a century. But as the **Titans** renew their attack, the world is expanded to create a frightening future scenario.

KAIJU NO. 8

One of the most popular manga of recent years, *Kaiju No. 8* is the creation of Matsumoto Naoya. A spectacular giant monster epic, the story follows Kafka Hibino as he becomes a Kaiju himself. He promises to use his new monstrous form as a force for good, while the Defense Force he joins has already dubbed his alter ego *Kaiju No. 8*. The saga remixes classic giant monster epics such as *Godzilla* into an exciting action adventure.

BREAKDOWN

▶ **Kafka Hibino** once dreamed of joining Japan's **Monster Defense Force**, fighting the many **Kaiju** attacking his homeland. While his childhood friend, **Ashiro Mina**, goes on to become one of the **Force's** leading members, **Kafka** fails to join and ends up working for a company that cleans up the hideous aftermath of battles. When **Kafka** swallows a small **Kaiju**, he finds himself transformed into a powerful creature—named Kaiju No. 8 by the **Defense Force**. **Kafka** decides to use his new power to fight monsters—even though his new allies in the **Defense Force** are hunting his alter ego.

SNAPSHOT

▶ **Matsumoto Naoya** was born in 1982. He worked as an assistant under **Iwashiro Toshiaki** before creating his own manga. His first series *Neko Wappa!* was published in *Weekly Shōnen Jump* from 2009 and his second, *Pochi Kuro* (PICTURED), in *Shōnen Jump+* from 2014. The latter series saw a girl trying to escape from a demonic realm only for a demon to fall in love with her. Matsumoto went on to create *Kaiju No. 8* for *Shōnen Jump+* in 2020.

THE CORE

MANGA

PUBLISHED BY: Shueisha
8 volumes, 2020–
WRITER/ARTIST:
Matsumoto Naoya

ANIME

PRODUCED FOR:
Studio Khara 2024

KAIJU

▶ **Kaiju** are giant monsters, a staple of manga. In *Kaiju No. 8*, the monsters come in all shapes and sizes, and are most abundant around Japan. When a monster is hard to kill, it is given a number by the **Defense Force**.

MONSTER SWEEPER INC.

▶ The brave heroes who fight the **Kaiju** might get all the glory, but someone must clean up the mess they leave behind. That's where companies like **Monster Sweeper Inc**. come in. Originally **Kafka** works as a cleaner for the company. Cleaning up dead monsters is hard work, and the dirtiest bit is dealing with their intestinal tract—a part of the job so gross that it's often censored in the manga.

JAPAN DEFENSE FORCE

Japan's main protection against rampaging monsters, the **Defense Force** are highly trained in fighting the various monsters threatening the country. Armed with high-tech weaponry, they are heroes to many. Notable members include:

▶ ASHIRO MINA

Kafka's childhood friend and the best female fighter in the **Defense Force**, **Mina** is a serious but caring person who once made a vow to defeat every **Kaiju** she could. She is captain of the **Third Division Defense Force**.

▶ GENERAL SHINOMIYA

Shinomiya Isao is the director general of the **Defense Force**, with years of experience behind him. He was once captain of the **First Division**. The father of **Kikoru**, **Isao** became distant and cold following his wife's death during a **Kaiju** attack.

▶ SHINOMIYA KIKORU

The daughter of **General Shinomiya** and a talented fighter, **Kikoru** seeks to kill as many **Kaiju** as she can following the death of her mother. The loss she experienced makes her push herself very hard to be the best she can.

▶ GENERAL NARUMI

As general of the **First Division**, **General Narumi** is regarded as one of Japan's best **Kaiju** fighters. Outside of combat, he can come across as somewhat spoiled and lazy.

▶ ICHIKAWA LENO

Leno worked briefly with **Kafka** at **Monster Sweeper Inc.** before joining the **Defense Force** and its **Third Division**.

MONSTER FIGHTING TECH
▶ Most of the **Defense Force's** high-tech weaponry is created by **Izumo Tech**—sometimes from the corpses of defeated **Kaiju**. From their high-tech battle suits to personalized weaponry, **Izumo Tech's** equipment is essential for the fight against the **Kaiju**.

ANIME ACTION
▶ The manga incarnation of *Kaiju No. 8* is going from strength to strength, with over **10 million copies** in circulation as the story continues. An anime adaptation is due for release in 2024 from **Production I.G.**, perhaps best known for *Ghost In the Shell* (PICTURED). There's a trailer online.

WHERE NEXT?
If you enjoy *Kaiju No. 8*, try these other monstrous epics:

▶ **DARLING IN THE FRANXX**
Set in a dystopian future where children are specially created to fight dark forces and violent monsters.

▶ **FULLMETAL ALCHEMIST: BROTHERHOOD (PICTURED)**
Two brothers use alchemy to take on evil in this dark fantasy manga that packs an emotional punch.

▶ **BLACK CLOVER**
In this exciting fantasy story filled with epic storytelling, **Asta** fights to become a hero in a world filled with magic.

YONA OF THE DAWN

(Akatsuki no Yona)

Yona of the Dawn is one of the best action fantasies available in shōjo manga (manga aimed at girls). Sometimes known as *Yona: The First Blush of Dawn*, the saga follows 16-year-old Yona as she goes from a naive princess to a heroic warrior following the murder of her father. The story mixes high drama with epic fantasy as only the best shōjo manga can!

BREAKDOWN

▶ **Princess Yona** is the only child of **King Il of Kouka**. She lives a privileged life inside her castle home—a life that's changed forever when she witnesses her beloved cousin **Su-won** murder her father. She flees with the help of her best friend and protector **Son-Hak** and soon learns that the best hope for her kingdom is to locate four mythical **Dragon warriors**.

SNAPSHOT

▶ **Kusanagi Mizuho** was born in 1979 and was the assistant to **Matsushita Yoko**. Her first series was *Yoiko no Kokoroe*, published in the shōjo magazine *Hana to Yuma* from 2003. **Kusanagi** has been a regular contributor ever since. She created *Yona of the Dawn* in 2009 and saw her series adapted into a successful anime series in 2014.

THE CORE
MANGA
PUBLISHED BY: Hakusensha
40 volumes, 2009–
WRITER/ARTIST: Kusanagi Mizuho
ANIME
PRODUCED BY: Pierrot
WRITER: Inotsume Shinichi
24 episodes and 3 OVAs

HEROES AND VILLAINS

▶ **YONA** Yona was raised by her pacifist father **King II**. She disliked her red hair and was in love with her cousin **Su-won**, who comforted her following her mother's death.

▶ **SON HAK** The dark-haired **Son Hak** is **Yona's** childhood friend and bodyguard. He was also the **General of the Wind Tribe** and called "Lightning Beast" due to his exceptional skill and speed in combat.

▶ **SU-WON** While technically the villain of the piece after killing **King II** in front of **Yona**, **Su-won** proves to be a good king. He later uses his authority to protect **Yona** and **Son Hak**.

THE DRAGONS

Yona's quest leads her to find the descendants of the **Dragon Gods**.

▶ **KIJA** Descendant and inheritor of the **White Dragon's claws**. These claws can grow amazingly large and cut through armor.

▶ **SHIN-AH** Descendant and inheritor of the **Blue Dragon's eyes**. He can see great distances and create horrific hallucinations and even heart attacks in those he uses his powerful gaze on.

▶ **JAE-HA** Descendant and inheritor of the **Green Dragon's right leg**. He has infinite strength in his leg and can use it to leap great distances or kick through armor.

▶ **ZENO** The original **Yellow Dragon**. The only survivor of the original **Dragon Gods**, his gift is immortality . . . and the wisdom his great age brings.

WHERE NEXT?

If you love *Yona of the Dawn*, try:

▶ **THE MYSTERIOUS PLAY (FUSHIGI YUGI)** Legends and friendship clash when two friends are transported back to ancient Japan by a mysterious book.

HOW TO DRAW . . .

ACTION

Ready for some ninja training? Follow these simple steps to draw your own dynamic young martial-arts student.

STEP 1

Using light pencil marks, indicate the motion of your character with a curving stick figure. The left hand pushes forward so it appears as large as the head.

STEP 2

Use blocky shapes to give the body form. Begin adding detail to the head, with eyes halfway down.

STEP 3

Fill out the figure, adding joints, plus the outline of his clothing. The ninja's spiky hair sprouts from the middle of his forehead.

STEP 4

Finish off your ninja by adding dynamic creases to his clothes that follow the movement of his body. Shape his fingers and add a nose and confident smirk to his face.

BLACK CLOVER

(Burakku Kurōbā)

Black Clover is an epic fantasy about a boy with no magical powers of his own—in a world where everyone has mystical abilities. Serialized in *Weekly Shōnen Jump* since 2015, *Black Clover* is one of the magazine's most popular features—adapted into anime, movies, books, and games. A mix of Harry Potter, The Lord of the Rings, and *Naruto*, it's a magical delight.

BREAKDOWN

▶ **Asta** and **Yuno** are two orphans who grew up together in a world filled with magic. At 15 everyone gets their own grimoire except for **Asta**, whose complete lack of magical powers makes him something of an outcast. While **Asta** eventually gets his own grimoire—one that provides him with amazing weapons—there is far more to the story than it seems, and it could corrupt the young hero. The saga follows both friends as they strive to become the **Wizard King**—facing some of the cruelest demonic villains in manga along the way.

SNAPSHOT

▶ **Tabata Yūki** submitted his first manga, *Hakamori*, to the 2001 **Tenkaichi Manga Awards** and received a special jury prize. His first professionally published work was *Hungry Joker* (PICTURED) published in *Weekly Shōnen Jump* and popular enough to be turned into a series in 2011. *Black Clover* also started life as a one-shot published on *Shōnen Jump Next!* before launching as a full series in 2015. Since then, it has become one of the most popular manga in Japan.

NEWTON ACHIEV[E] THE KNOWLEDG[E] OF HIS *LAW O[F] UNIVERSAL GRAVITATION[?]

THE CORE
MANGA
PUBLISHED BY: Shueisha
33 volumes, 2015–
WRITER/ARTIST: Tabata Yūki
SPIN-OFFS
Black Clover AD: Asta Kun's Road to the Wizard King 2018–2021
Black Clover side story: Quartet Knights 2018–2020
ANIME
PRODUCED FOR: Pierrot 2017–2021
170 episodes
MOVIE
Black Clover: Sword of the Wizard King
PRODUCED FOR: Netflix

MAGICAL RIVALS

▶ **Asta** and **Yono** both want to be the **Wizard King**. As the series begins, **Yono** seems to have the head start—he's a prodigy with exceptional magical abilities, and he's even selected to have a special **four-leaf clover grimoire**. He's tall, good-looking, and confident. **Asta** eventually gets a grimoire of his own—a special five-leaf one supposedly linked to devils.

BOOK DAY!

▶ In the world of *Black Clover*, when would-be mages reach 15, they gain a **magical grimoire**. The **grimoire** is connected to **Mana**, the source of magic in *Black Clover*. **Mana** exists in all things—including people—as a sort of spiritual force. It can be controlled and used in magic spells, with the **grimoires** enabling mages to use spells far greater than their normal ability would allow.

MAGIC KNIGHTS

▶ The **Clover Kingdom** is protected by nine squads of warrior mages known as the **Magic Knights**. Each squad has its own name—**Golden Dawn, Black Bull, Silver Eagle, Blue Rose, Crimson Lion, Green Mantis, Coral Peacock, Purple Orca**, and **Aqua Deer**. Stars are awarded to knights for good performance and heroic deeds, while black stars are awarded for failure and poor performance. The **Wizard King** (PICTURED) watches over the knights below him. The knights have four ranks—**Grand Magic Knights, Senior Knights, Intermediate Knights**, and **Junior Knights**. Each class has five levels from first to fifth level (first is the highest). **Yuno** ends up as a member of the **Golden Dawn**, and **Asta** a **Black Bull**.

SPIN-OFFS

Black Clover's success has led to some cool spin-off series.

▶ **BLACK CLOVER AD: ASTA KUN'S ROAD TO THE WIZARD KING** A comedy series illustrated by **Kobayashi Setta** follows **Asta** trying to become the **Wizard King**. It was published in *Saikyō Jump* and later reprinted in three collections.

▶ **BLACK CLOVER SIDE STORY: QUARTET KNIGHTS** Illustrated by **Tashiro Yumiya** and originally published on *Shōnen Jump+*, it retold the story of the computer game and was later collected into six volumes.

▶ **MAGICAL ANIME** *Black Clover* became a popular anime in 2017 while an OVA was also made. The movie *Black Clover: Sword of the Wizard King* appeared on Netflix in 2023. There was also a spin-off series created in the chibi design named *Squishy! Black Clover* (PICTURED).

WHERE NEXT?

If you like *Black Clover*, try:

▶ **RADIANT** (PICTURED)
Like *Black Clover*, there's a lot of magic in *Radiant*—only in this series, magic falls from the sky. When **monstrous Nemeses** fall to Earth, they mutate people they touch, leaving them with magical abilities. The hero, **Seth**, hopes to use his new skills to bring peace to the land.

▶ **MAGI: THE LABYRINTH OF MAGIC**
Another magical world, but in this one, anybody who can conquer magical dungeons can become as powerful as a king. A great cast and great action make this a must-read.

▶ **FAIRY TAIL**
Like *Black Clover*, it's a world filled with magic. Only in this world, instead of **Magic Knights**, there are sorcerers guilds. The story follows a mage named **Lucy** as she tries to overcome a curse with some allies and friends.

TOP 10
ANIME COUPLES

W ho are the anime couples that were truly made for each other? From high school sweethearts to ninja teammates and time-travelers, here is our pick of the most touching twosomes whose partnerships we can't resist.

1 STEINS;GATE

OKABE RINTARŌ & MAKISE KURISU

▶ It's a love that crosses time and space. After self-confessed "mad scientist" **Okabe Rintarō** and his friends find a way to send text messages back through time it leads to them saving the life of researcher **Makise Kurisu**. But, when a global research team claim their tech, **Rintarō** has to unravel the changes they made to time in order to save his best friend—all while risking **Kurisu's** death. **Rintarō** and **Kurisu** start out as quarrelsome lab colleagues, but the pair fall for each other through their mutual love of science. This complex sci-fi thriller has a budding romance at its heart— one that the peril of world war and multiple timelines threatens to destroy.

2 — FULLMETAL ALCHEMIST: BROTHERHOOD

EDWARD ELRIC & WINRY ROCKBELL

▶ Born out of tragedy, the relationship between **Edward** and **Winry** has moved from compassion to passion. When **Edward** loses his arm and leg in a failed transmutation experiment (see page 146), his 11-year-old friend **Winry** designs artificial replacements. **Winry** is a trained surgeon and automail mechanic who sticks by **Edward**, providing tech and emotional support while he seeks to restore his brother **Alphonse's** soul. They are both stubborn and independent, but their bickering only makes it clear just how much they care for each other's safety. Do they finally open up about their feelings for each other? You have to watch to the end of the series to find out.

3 — NARUTO

UZUMAKI NARUTO & HYŪGA HINATA

▶ If you're a fan of the follow-up, *Boruto: Naruto Next Generations*, you'll know how this pairing turns out. **Hinata's** crush on **Naruto** begins on his first day at **Ninja Academy**, when **Naruto** saves her from bullies. But, while focused on training, **Naruto** pays little attention to the soft-spoken girl. Over time, **Naruto's** eyes are opened. He sees how **Hinata** is willing to risk her life for his, and he becomes more protective of her and even reveals his insecurities.

4 — SWORD ART ONLINE

KIRIGAYA KIRITO & ASUNA YUUKI

▶ **Kirigaya Kazuto** ("**Kirito**") and **Asuna Yuuki** meet in a virtual-reality adventure where players cannot log out unless they beat a hundred levels of the lethal game. **Kirito** is a game-tester and is able to find out the in-game identity of the game's creator so that they can stop him and free themselves. As they fight for their lives, the duo develop an unbreakable bond. With each moment threatening to be their last, **Kirito** and **Yuuki** waste no time and decide to marry and honeymoon within the game. Then they finally meet in the real world.

5 INUYASHA
INUYASHA & HIGURASHI KAGOME

▶ In this classic fantasy adventure, high school girl **Higurashi Kagome** gets transported to the past where she teams up with half-demon-half-dog hero, **Inuyasha**. **Kagome** is the reincarnation of **Inuyasha's** lost love, **Kikyō**. Despite her resemblance, Inuyasha is aware she is a different person. As with many of the couples on this list, the pair argue at first but only out of concern. After a long adventure, **Kagome** is finally returned to her time, but her attachment to **Inuyasha** remains. Three years later, she has the opportunity to make the leap back in time, and she jumps at the chance to reunite with **Inuyasha**.

6 CLANNAD
OKAZAKI TOMOYA & FURUKAWA NAGISA

▶ The rebellious boy and the shy, considerate girl falling for each other is a cliché in anime, but it is done well in *Clannad*. **Okazaki Tomoya** is in his third year at high school and is totally disillusioned with study. He meets **Furukawa Nagisa**, who is retaking her third year after an illness that kept her out of school. She lacks confidence, and he lacks positivity. Together they work behind the scenes for a drama club and recognize that they belong together. The story continues beyond graduation in the sequel, *Clannad: After Story*, but a happy ending is not certain.

7 FRUITS BASKET
HONDA TŌRU & SŌMA KYO

▶ When orphaned high school girl **Honda Tōru** is discovered camping on the grounds of the **Sōma family estate**, she is swiftly adopted by the household. She accidentally discovers their secret—that they are cursed to take the form of zodiac animals when wet or stressed. At first it seems **Tōru** will fall under the spell of her classmate **Sōma Yuki** (the zodiac rat). They do become close, but it's his brother **Kyo** (the zodiac cat) who captures her heart. **Kyo** is short-tempered and resists **Tōru's** efforts to interact, but they do eventually open up to each other.

8 YOUR NAME. (KIMI NO NA WA)

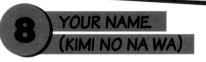

TACHIBANA TAKI & MIYAMIZU MITSUHA

▶ In an unusual take on a high school romance, the movie *Your Name.* follows small-town student **Miyamizu Mitsuha** and Tokyo schoolboy **Tachibana Taki** as they swap bodies for no apparent reason. They must then live the other's life for a while. They learn to communicate with each other by leaving messages, and both try to improve each other's lives, even fixing dates. As the pair increasingly care for each other, **Taki** tries to seek out **Mitsuha**. What he discovers leads him on an important mission, but we won't spoil the ending!

9 ORANGE

NARUSE KAKERU & TAKAMIYA NAHO

▶ Ready for more time-mangling romance? **Takamiya Naho** is a shy Tokyo high school girl who receives letters from her future self. These letters describe events to come, including details of her falling in love with a transfer student named **Naruse Kakeru**. The letters warn of a tragedy that could befall **Kakeru**, compelling **Naho** to come out of her shell and do her best to change the future. The situation becomes more complex when **Naho's** friends also receive letters from their future selves, but it is the honest feelings shared by **Kakeru** and **Naho** that ground the fantasy premise.

10 DUSK MAIDEN OF AMNESIA

KANOE YUUKO & NIIYA TEIICHI

▶ Could you fall for a ghost? **Niiya Teiichi** is a member of a school **paranormal club** investigating rumors that the spirit of a dead girl haunts **Seikyou Private Academy**. Sure enough, **Teiichi** discovers the ghost of **Kanoe Yuuko** . . . and she's adorable. The pair become inseparable, but **Yuuko** has a troubled past that she has no memory of. The relationship between **Yuuko** and his new friend is bittersweet, and the resolution of their story equally so.

THAT TIME I GOT REINCARNATED AS A SLIME

(TenSura)

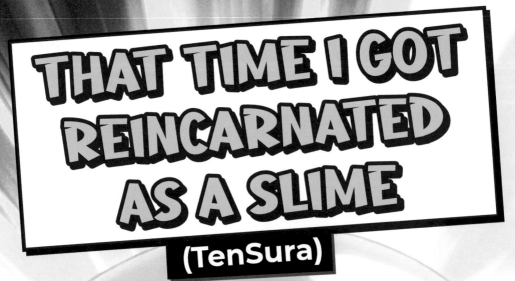

G ot time for slime? Mikami Satoru makes the best out of dying and being reborn as a powerful blob. Soon he's ruling a kingdom and taking on all comers in this hugely popular fantasy adventure.

BREAKDOWN

▶ **Mikami Satoru** is just your average office worker until . . . he suffers an unexpected attack and wakes up in a fantasy world in the body of a large **Slime**—a blob with powers. The Slime can absorb the skills and take on the appearance of other creatures. The Slime is given the name **Rimuru** by a dragon, then claims the dragon's powers and many more magical abilities. He is soon taken on as the ruler of a Goblin Village in the **Great Forest of Jura**. As alliances are formed, this expands into the nation of **Tempest**. From a simple-looking Slime, a wise leader is born, but enemies soon gather to steal his crown.

SNAPSHOT

▶ **Fuse** is the pen name for the writer of *That Time I Got Reincarnated as a Slime*. A former construction worker, **Fuse** first published **Rimuru's** story online in 2013. It was then picked up by *Micro Magazine* as a series of 20 light novels (so far) and illustrated by **Vah Mitz**. **Fuse** describes the story as being about **"just doing what you can"** in extraordinary circumstances. He also says that **Rimuru** is his image of the ideal boss. The book series was picked up for a TV anime adaptation in 2018 with a spin-off, *The Slime Diaries*, launching in 2021, plus five manga spin-offs and a movie.

THE CORE
MANGA
PUBLISHED BY: Kodansha, 20 volumes, plus 5 spin-off series 2015–2022
WRITER: Fuse
ARTIST: Kawakami Taiki
ANIME
PRODUCED FOR: Eight Bit, 2018–
WRITER: Fudeyasu Kazuyuki
48 episodes, 5 OVAs, plus spin-off *The Slime Diaries*
MOVIE
That Time I Got Reincarnated as a Slime: Scarlet Bond 2022

SKILL PROFILE

▶ **Mikami Satoru** soon discovers that his Slime profile enables him to **pick up skills** as if he's in a video game. One of the first is **"Predator,"** which is the ability to ingest objects, gain their skills, and then duplicate them. He uses this to free the storm dragon, **Veldora**, from his prison before tackling a cave serpent with a new **Water Blade skill** and slicing off its neck. After various attempts at mimicking another body, **Rimuru** settles on that of an outsider, **Shizu** (known as the Conqueror of Flames) (PICTURED). He presents himself in her androgynous form with long, dark silvery hair, and sometimes sporting dragon wings.

WHERE NEXT?

If you love *That Time I Got Reincarnated as a Slime*, try:

▶ **LOG HORIZON** (PICTURED)
Log Horizon features a regular guy, like **Satoru**, in the form of a student named **Shiroe**. He's dropped into a fantasy realm, the RPG *Elder Tale*, to act as a leader, and he's joined by 30,000 other players!

▶ **THE DEVIL IS A PART-TIMER!**
Flipping the convention, this 2013 anime has **Satan** landing in modern-day Japan and taking a job in a fast-food restaurant, among other comedic adventures.

RANKING OF KINGS
(Ōsama Rankingu)

Ranking of Kings appears to be the adorable adventures of a tiny prince and his strange companion. But there is plenty of court intrigue and danger on display as rivals vie for the throne of the Bosse Kingdom.

BREAKDOWN

▶ Young **Prince Bojii** was born **deaf**, and he dreams of becoming a great king. His best friend is a strange dark blob named **Kage** (the last survivor of an assassin clan), who is able to understand the nonverbal prince. When **Bojii's** father (**King Bosse**) dies, the throne is grabbed by **Bojii's** younger half-brother, **Prince Daida**. Determined **Bojii** goes on an adventure with **Kage** to gain knowledge and strength in order to claim his right and ability to rule in his father's stead.

SNAPSHOT

▶ **Tōka Sōsuke** started out late in the world of manga. In fact, *Ranking of Kings* was his debut at the age of 41, after years of working in an office. Even when the series was successfully adapted for anime, **Tōka** kept the news that he had quit his salaried job from his parents!

THE CORE

MANGA

PUBLISHED BY: Echoes, Enterbrain, 15 volumes 2017–
WRITER/ARTIST: Tōka Sōsuke

ANIME

PRODUCED BY: Wit Studio, 2021–2022
WRITER: Kishimoto Taku
23 episodes

CURSED CHILD

▶ Before **Bojii's** birth, the **Bosse Kingdom** was threatened by a tribe of monsters. In order to defeat them, the giant **King Bosse** had to make a pact with a demon, taking the power of his firstborn to give him the strength to conquer the monsters. While the war was won, it meant that **Bojii** was born tiny, weak, and deaf.

DARK COMPANION

▶ **Bojii's** friend **Kage** (meaning "shadow") appears as a dark puddle with eyes. As a member of the **Shadow Clan**, **Kage** is cursed to inhabit a liquid body, but this allows him to sneak across floors and walls, hiding in the shadows. He can sprout limbs and a mouth when needed, and even go giant-size when angry.

▶ **Kage** was a child when he saw his family wiped out. He managed to escape and use his talents to survive through thieving. He meets **Bojii** when he steals from him but is soon moved by **Bojii's** natural kindness. Aggrieved by the prince's mistreatment by the royal court, **Kage** decides to become the young prince's friend and bodyguard.

WHERE NEXT?

If you love *Ranking of Kings*, try:

▶ **DORORO** (PICTURED)
Written by the late, great **Tezuka Osamu** (see page 108), *Dororo* follows the quest of a boy lacking features, organs, and limbs who fights for their return from a series of demons.

▶ **KAIBA**
Featuring charming animation, *Kaiba* centers around a young man who wakes with a hole in his heart and a locket holding the picture of a mysterious girl. He must go on a quest to recover his past.

FULLMETAL ALCHEMIST

A steampunk classic, *Fullmetal Alchemist* is one of anime's most successful franchises.

This thrilling manga has sold 80 million volumes, spawning two anime series, several video games, a range of action figures, plus three live-action movies.

BREAKDOWN

▶ Brothers **Edward** and **Alphonse Elric** longed to be reunited with their dead mother. Using their training in alchemy, they attempt transmutation, but their experiment fails, and it leaves **Edward** missing his left leg, and **Alphonse** lost altogether. **Edward** sacrifices his right arm to bring back **Alphonse's soul** and bind it to a **suit of armor**. Despite the failure, the **Elrics'** alchemic skills are recognized by **Colonel Roy Mustang** who enrolls them to train to become **State Alchemists** (with Edward gaining the moniker of **Fullmetal**). While **Edward** replaces his missing limbs with automail prosthetics, he is determined to restore his brother. To do this he needs to find the legendary **Philosopher's Stone** . . .

ARTISTIC ALCHEMY

▶ **Arakawa Hiromu** grew up on a dairy farm in Hokkaidō, Japan, and dreamed of becoming a manga artist. Moving to Tokyo in 1999, she took up work as an assistant to **Etō Hiroyuki**, the creator of *Magical Circle Guru Guru* before getting her break with the award-winning story *Stray Dog*. **Arakawa's** interest in the mythical Philosopher's Stone and alchemy led to her to create *Fullmetal Alchemist*. The manga series launched in 2001 and ran for nine years. The first anime adaptation was completed before the manga and featured a different ending, approved by the author. The second series, *Fullmetal Alchemist: Brotherhood*, follows the manga more closely.

▶ Once *Fullmetal Alchemist* was completed, **Arakawa** worked on the historical fantasy *Hero Tales* and the slice-of-life manga *Silver Spoon*, which depicts or shows elements of **Arakawa's** agricultural upbringing. Both titles have been adapted for anime. In 2021, she launched the supernatural manga saga *Daemons of the Shadow Realm*.

THE CORE

MANGA
PUBLISHED BY: Enix, Square Enix,
27 volumes
2001–2010
WRITER/ARTIST: Arakawa Hiromu

ANIME
PRODUCED BY: Bones, 2003–2004
WRITER: Aikawa Shō
51 episodes
Fullmetal Alchemist: Brotherhood
PRODUCED BY: Bones, 2009–2010
WRITER: Ōnogi Hiroshi
64 episodes, 4 OVAs

MOVIES
Fullmetal Alchemist the Movie: Conqueror of Shamballa 2005
Fullmetal Alchemist: The Sacred Star of Milos 2011

ANCIENT ART

▶ In the country of **Amestris**, alchemy is the most significant of the sciences. **Mastery of alchemy** allows the user to change the properties of elements and use **transmutation circles** to create almost anything in exchange for a material of equal value (according to the **Law of Equivalent Exchange**). Transmutation of gold and humans is forbidden.

HEART OF STONE

▶ The **Philosopher's Stone** is said to allow its user to ignore the **Law of Equivalent Exchange** and transmute even human flesh without a trade-off. Unknown to the **Elrics**, it is a military creation that was built using human tissue. The stone is also wanted by the **Homunculi**—artificial humanoid creatures created through alchemy. The key **Homunculi** that threaten the **Elrics** are named after the seven deadly sins. These sins were purged from their leader, who was the centuries-old original Homunculus, known as **Father**.

AUTOMAIL UPGRADE

▶ The automotive metal prosthetics used by **Edward Elric** were designed by his friend **Winry**—they are known as **automail**. Automail connect directly to a body's nervous system, require no power source, and can be controlled in the same way as flesh. The installation process is painful, however, and requires a lot of recovery time. It took **Edward Elric** a year to become comfortable and accustomed to his prosthetics. **Automail customization** can involve the addition of **weaponry**, such as firearms, blades, and diamond-tipped claws. **Edward Elric's** knowledge of alchemy allows him to transmute his automail arm into a sword.

CONSPIRACY THEORIES

▶ **Edward** and **Alphonse** receive their alchemy training under the military, but they discover that the army of **Amestris** has a dark agenda. The authoritarian nation of **Amestris** (PICTURED) is based on 1920s Germany, with the aims of the army paralleling the rise of the Nazis. Other regions do exist in the world of *Fullmetal Alchemist*. Ishval is a province that resembles the Middle East, and Xing is a version of China. **Arakawa Hiromu's** brilliant world building weaves secret plans, conspiracies, and excellent characters into an adventure spanning years! It's one reason the series is so highly rated.

X MARKS THE SPOT

▶ In revenge for the genocide of his people, the Ishvalan vigilante, **Scar** (named for the X-shaped mark on his forehead), has targeted all **Amestris State Alchemists**. He attacks the **Elrics** more than once. As a former warrior-monk, **Scar** is combat trained and fast enough to dodge bullets, but his deadliest weapon is the powerful alchemist tattoo on his right arm. Once belonging to his older brother, the tattoo exploits the first two stages of transmutation—comprehension and deconstruction—without reconstruction. This ultimately means that **Scar** can destroy anyone with a touch.

LIVE TRILOGY

▶ Three live-action movies based on the original manga have been released— *Fullmetal Alchemist* (PICTURED) in 2017, and both *The Revenge of Scar* and *The Last Transmutation* in 2022—in celebration of the 20th anniversary of the original manga.

HOW TO DRAW . . .
MECHA

Test your technical drawing skills with this mega step-by-step build-up for a mighty mecha.

STEP 1

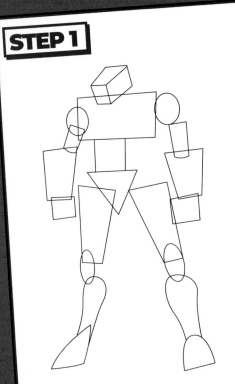

Using light pencil lines, build a basic jointed mecha body out of geometric shapes.

STEP 2

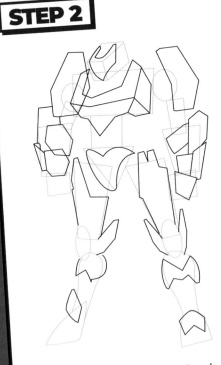

Now add armor over the basic shapes, especially over the chest, shoulders, and thighs. Keep the design symmetrical.

STEP 3

Begin adding mechanized detail, with round shoulder, elbow, and knee hinges. Design extended armor plating to cover the shoulders, upper legs, and feet.

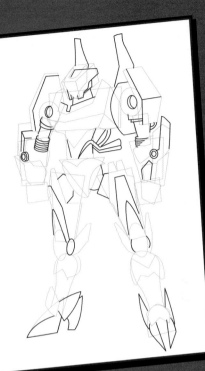

STEP 4

Add extra layers to the armor, following the original lines. Be sure to make the parts appear 3D, bulking up your figure so it looks unstoppable. Add extra cables and pipes to your figure wherever you like.

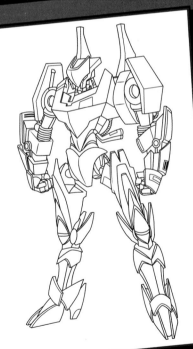

ROUNDED MECHA

Here's a different style of mecha you can try. Rather than blocky shapes, this figure is built with more rounded, organic shapes. The forearms and lower legs are especially bulky.

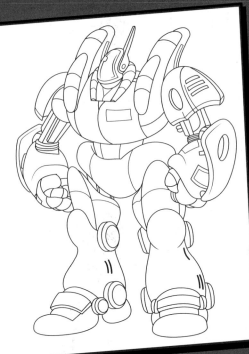

BUG MECHA

Mecha don't have to be human shaped. This flying robot is based on a wasp, but it's bound to have a more powerful sting.

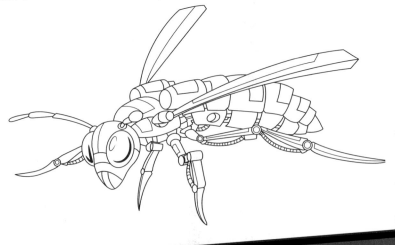

HINGES AND HYDROLICS

Here are some example parts you can add to your mecha design to provide motion and mechanical muscle.

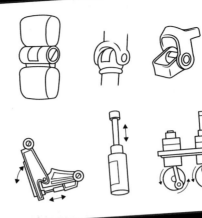

WEAPONS

When metal fists are not enough, why not weaponize your mecha with these suggestions:

How about a buzzsaw that can grind through metal?

Or a hidden laser sword that extends from the mecha's wrist plating?

Or a pneumatic spinning mace that will put your mecha's foes in their place?

KYOTO ANIMATION

Home of hugely popular slice-of-life and high school–set TV shows and movies, Kyoto Animation has been producing top-notch anime for almost 40 years.

BREAKDOWN

▶ **Kyoto Animation**, also known as **KyoAni**, began as a small group of dedicated friends and housewives under the name **Kyoto Anime Studio**. **KyoAni** is led by **Hatta Yôko**, who had previously worked as a painter at **Mushi Production**, the anime studio founded by **Tezuka Osamu** (see page 108). **Yôko's** team painted animation cels for shows such as *SDS Macross*, *Urusei Matsura*, and *Genesis Climber Mospeada*. In 1985, **Yôko** and her husband **Hideaki** set up **Kyoto Animation** as a limited company and expanded the business by taking on animation work for big-name series like *Neon Genesis Evangelion* (PICTURED TOP LEFT).

▶ The first major independent work produced by the studio was a season of the series *Full Metal Panic!* (PICTURED) in 2003, about a special-forces soldier acting as a bodyguard for a high school girl. From then on, **KyoAni** were able to mix commissioned work with their own projects, adapting light novels for anime. The studio focused on romantic and slice-of-life dramas rather than fantasy. Their first big hit was a series named *The Melancholy of Haruhi Suzumiya* (PICTURED TOP RIGHT).

SHARP FOCUS

▶ **KyoAni** impress with their attention to detail—including the smooth movement, subtlety, and intricate backgrounds in their animations. The backgrounds are often based on real-life locations that fans have been able to seek out. **KyoAni** mostly focus on high schools and students—only two of their productions don't feature students. By avoiding the drama of supernatural or martial-arts fight scenes, **KyoAni** can concentrate on the small things and the gentle moments between characters that reveal more of their personalities.

THE CORE

22 movies	
30 TV series	
9 OVAs	
2 web animations	

Highlights

Full Metal Panic! 2003, 2005
The Melancholy of Haruhi Suzumiya 2006, 2009
Lucky Star 2007
Clannad 2007–2008
K-On! 2009, 2010
Nichijou 2011
Love, Chunibyo & Other Delusions! 2012, 2014
A Silent Voice 2016
Miss Kobayashi's Dragon Maid 2017, 2021
Free! 2017, 2018, 2021, 2022
Violet Evergreen 2018–2020
Tsurune 2018, 2022, 2023

The melancholy of Haruhi Suzumiya

▶ While the industry is dominated by freelance talent and long working hours, **KyoAni** break the mold. They have a reputation for a more-relaxed working environment, full-time jobs, and less-stressful deadlines. Animators are also trained in-house.

FULL METAL PANIC!

AWARD HOSTS

▶ As well as creating some of the finest anime, **Kyoto Animation** has also hosted the **Kyoto Animation Awards** since 2009. The awards recognize the best in original novels, manga, and scenarios. Prizewinners have the chance to be published by the company or have their works adapted for anime. In 2014, the steampunk light novel *Violet Evergarden* became the first work to win the grand prize for a novel. It was adapted for a TV series in 2018, followed by two movies. Admired for its visuals and soundtrack, *Violet Evergarden* is the story of a former female soldier dealing with life outside of combat.

THE BAND PLAYS ON

▶ While there are several popular anime featuring teenagers forming pop and rock bands—including **KyoAni's** own *K-On!*— *Sound! Euphonium (Hibike! Euphonium)* (PICTURED) follows the fortunes of a high-school orchestra. Led by four female players, **Kumiko**, **Reina**, **Sapphire**, and **Hazuki**, the series begins with characters picking their instruments and following instruction from the school's new music teacher who is trying to improve the class so it can compete at the national level. Based on a series of novels by **Takeda Ayano**, the series has gained praise for its accurate portrayal of music classes and performance, as well as its likeable characters. **KyoAni** have produced two anime series and two movies so far, and there's a third expected in 2024.

DIVING IN

▶ *Free!* (PICTURED) is based on the Kyoto Animation–published novel *High Speed!* by **Ouji Kouji**. This sports anime is set in the world of competitive swimming. Teenager **Haru** is the main protagonist—a naturally talented swimmer who revives his school's swimming club with a group of friends to take on rival schools. The series was **KyoAni's** first sports anime and first show to feature a predominantly male cast—although it's aimed at a female audience. It is a huge hit—with two seasons and seven movies produced (so far!) over nine years. **KyoAni** have since followed it up with anime adaptations of the archery-based light novel series, *Tsurune* (2018–), a new series of which premiered early in 2023.

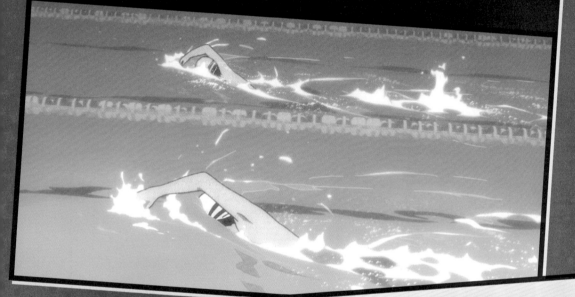

SILENT TREATMENT

▶ One of the studio's biggest international hits was the 2016 movie *A Silent Voice (Koe no Katachi)*. **KyoAni's** talent for expressing emotion through body language was pivotal in this story as it was based on a character with a hearing impairment. Based on the manga by **Ōima Yoshitoki**, the movie tells the story of teenager **Ishida Shōya** who tries to make up for his bullying ways in elementary school by befriending his target, **Nishimiya Shōko**—a hearing-impaired former classmate. Through his attempts to behave more considerately, **Ishida** gains redemption. The movie won the prize for Best Animated Feature Film at the 26th Japanese Movie Critics Awards, and director **Yamada Naoko** received special praise.

TOP 10

ANIME RIVALRIES

W hat's a hero without a rival to butt heads against? Here's our pick of 10 classic contenders for the win, the prize, the girl, the boy . . . or just the claim to be top dog.

1 MY HERO ACADEMIA

MIDORIYA IZUKU vs. BAKUGO KATSUKI

▶ **Katsuki** is convinced of his own greatness and bullies **Izuku** at school for his lack of a **Quirk**. When **Izuku** dares to enroll in the **Hero Program** at U.A. High School, it's another excuse for **Bakugo** to be mean to the hero fanboy. The rivalry grows stronger when **Izuku** finally gains the power of **One for All**, courtesy of **All Might**, and **Bakugo** is fired up with jealousy. The pair fight many times but—as often happens with anime rivals—they slowly gain respect for each other and join forces to tackle more important foes.

2 DRAGON BALL

VEGETA vs. GOKU

▶ Just like **Izuku** and **Bakugo**, **Vegata** and **Goku** have a grudging respect for each other but also a desire to come out on top. They meet as enemies when **Prince Vegeta** arrives on Earth with the aim of destroying it. **Vegeta** is outraged when he is defeated by the "lower-class" Saiyan and attempts to prove himself as better whenever possible. Eventually they become friends that train together to tackle powerful foes as a team. Their rivalry is then passed on to their children, **Goten** and **Trunks**.

3 FRUITS BASKET

SŌMA YUKI vs. SŌMA KYO

▶ The **cat** and the **rat** have been rivals since the **legend of the zodiac**, when the feline is excluded from the zodiac pantheon due to the rat's deception. This animosity rolls over in *Fruits Basket*, with their human embodiments, **Sōma Yuki** and **Sōma Kyo**, at odds. **Kyo** is excluded from the zodiac group and takes out his resentment on **Yuki** (several times). But he is the ultimate victor as he claims the heart of **Honda Tōru**.

4 FOOD WARS!

YUKIHIRA SŌMA vs. NAKIRI ERINA

▶ The underdog taking on the champion is typical of anime rivalries. When diner chef **Yukihira Sōma** arrives at the elite culinary school **Tōtsuki Academy**, he is looked down upon by gourmet student **Nakiri Erina**. But **Sōma's** untraditional cooking methods and use of simple ingredients surprises and impresses his school rival who presumes only high-class restaurant food is worthy. In this case, the rivals battle with feasts rather than fists.

5 NARUTO

UZUMAKI NARUTO vs. UCHIHA SASUKE

▶ A classic anime rivalry, **Naruto** and **Sasuke** face off from their first year at **ninja school**. They have lots in common but see each other as competition. Both the easy-going **Naruko** and the arrogant **Sasuke** are equally talented. **Sasuke** becomes obsessed with vengeance and turns to the dark to gain power. He even threatens to kill **Naruto**, while his school teammate seeks to redeem him. It all comes to a head with the battle at the **Valley of the End** when the duo is finally reconciled. A more mature **Sasuke** appears in *Boruto: Naruto Next Generations* as the mentor to Naruto's son.

6 KAGUYA-SAMA: LOVE IS WAR

SHINOMIYA KAGUYA vs. SHIROGANE MIYUKI

▶ Meet **Shuchiin Academy** rivals—student council president **Shirogane Miyuki** and vice president **Shinomiya Kaguya**. As the top two in their classes, they compete against each other through academic work. But their main aim is to force the other to show they care and to confess their love. Pride sure gets in the way as neither of them wants to be first to admit their feelings. **Kaguya** wants to prove her ability with top grades, and **Miyuki** believes **Kaguya** won't love or respect him unless he scores highest.

7 ASSASSINATION CLASSROOM

SHIOTA NAGISA vs. AKABANE KARMA

▶ In a rather wacky premise, a monstrous tentacled creature destroys most of the Moon, then threatens the same fate for Earth. The creature assumes the form of a teacher, nicknamed **"Koro-sensei,"** and trains a class of junior high school students to be assassins. With a reward on his head, the creature becomes the seemingly invincible target of his students. **Shiota Nagisa** and **Akabane Karma** are two resourceful classmates aiming for the top spot among a class of delinquent amateur killers. Who will deliver the fatal blow?

8 POKÉMON

ASH KETCHUM vs. GARY OAK

▶ The far-from-neighborly Pallet Town boys, **Ash Ketchum** and **Gary Oak**, have been battling to become Pokémon master for years. **Gary** is the grandson of Pokémon expert **Professor Oak**. He plays the arrogant role here, putting down poor **Ash** and collecting most of the Pokémon while **Ash** creeps up the league. Naturally, the rivals put their differences aside after one big battle.

9 FAIRY TAIL

NATSU DRAGNEEL vs. GAJEEL REDFOX

▶ Fellow **Dragon Slayers** drawn from 400 years in the past, **Natsu** and **Gajeel** are supposed to be on the same side but often trade barbs and blows. **Natsu** is a **Fire Dragon Slayer**, whereas **Gajeel** is **Iron**. While they often bait each other, they will stand up for each other when it counts. **Gajeel** notably saves **Natsu** from an attack by **Laxus Dreyer**.

10 YU-GI-OH!

MUTO YUGI vs. KAIBA SETO

▶ *Yu-Gi-Oh!* features two combatants with similar abilities but very different personalities. They face each other in regular competitions with alternating wins. **Muto Yugi** and **Kaiba Seto** are card-playing rivals in the game of **Duel Monsters**—for them, this is a war of heart against power. Despite their differences, they do gain respect for each other's skills as Duelists and come together on occasion to fight shared enemies, such as **Marik Ishtar**.

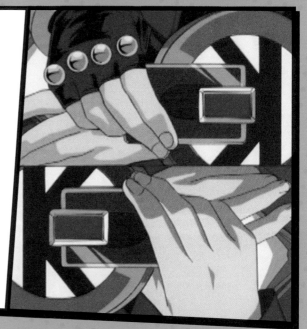

GINTAMA

A sci-fi samurai comedy mash-up, *Gintama* has it all with sword-wielding heroes, out-of-time tech, alien invaders, gigantic dogs, and heaps of laughs.

BREAKDOWN

▶ When (a version of) late-19th-century Earth comes under alien attack, Japan's samurai stand ready to fight the extraterrestrial threat. They do this until their leadership, the shōgun, surrender and ban the carrying of swords in public. Under the alien occupation, former samurai **Sakata Gintoki** must find other ways to make a living. Along with teen trainee samurai **Shimura Shinpachi** and rescued superstrong alien girl, **Kagura**, he sets up a freelance agency. He calls it **"Yorozuya"** (which means "we do everything"). Their work ranges from locating lost kittens to saving the world. Rarely does anything go to plan.

SNAPSHOT

▶ **Sorachi Hideaki** is the pen name for the writer/artist on *Gintama*. He took his name from the Sorachi prefecture in Hokkaidō, Japan, where he grew up. Inspired by reading manga and watching movies such as **Studio Ghibli's** (see page 72) *Castle in the Sky*, **Sorachi** took up drawing. After studying for a degree in advertising, **Sorachi** sent off his first manga work to a publisher. This work was the one-shot *Dandelion*, and it was accepted and published in 2002. Encouraged, **Sorachi** began work on *Gintama*. The series was a slow burner, which steadily built a fan base over months. It eventually lasted for 16 years, with 55 million copies of the collected volumes sold. As for the title's genre, **Sorachi** described it as **"science fiction human drama pseudo-historical comedy."**

THE CORE
MANGA
PUBLISHED BY: Shueisha, 77 volumes, 2003–2019
WRITER/ARTIST: Sorachi Hideaki

ANIME
PRODUCED BY: Sunrise, 2006–2013
Bandai Namco Pictures, 2015–2018
WRITERS: Yamatoya Akatsuki, Akao Deko, Matsubara Shū, Kishimoto Taku, Tachihara Masaki
367 episodes, 2 OVAs

MOVIES
Gintama: The Movie 2010
Gintama: The Movie: The Final Chapter: Be Forever Yorozuya 2013
Gintama: The Very Final 2021

SHIROYASHA

▶ **Sakata Gintoki** is a skilled samurai who fought in the **Joui War** against the alien invaders. During the war he became known as **Shiroyasha** (white demon) for his silver hair, white clothing, and devilish swordsmanship. As a member of the **Yorozuya**, he is rather lazy. He prefers to read manga, particularly the Japanese weekly magazine *Shōnen Jump*, which *Gintama* appears in. He also loves eating sweet food (especially chocolate parfait with strawberry milk). **Gintoki** throws any money he has on the game **Pachinko**. As a result, he is usually behind on his rent and eager to avoid his landlady, Otose. While confident in battle, there is one thing **Gintoki** is known to be afraid of . . . ghosts.

THE SKY PEOPLE

▶ The varied aliens that take over Earth in *Gintama* are known as the "Amanto" or "Sky People." They had fought wars over a planetary life force known as **Altana**. This led one group of wealthy aliens to invade Earth for quantities of the power source emerging from late-Edo period Japan. Overwhelmed by the aliens' superior power, the Japanese government capitulated. This led to a civil war. The resistance group known as the **Joui** opposed the alien takeover, and the **Amanto** became more involved in Japanese affairs.

The **Amanto** have various forms—some resembling **humans**, some **canine bipeds**, some **horned demons**, and then there's the **Renho Tribe** who wear cartoon duck costumes (PICTURED)!

▶ Thanks to **Amanto** influence, late-19th-century Japan in *Gintama* contains more recent technology, including scooters, skyscrapers, and the aliens' own faster-than-light spaceships.

ON PATROL

▶ The **Shinsengumi** were originally going to be the main focus of *Gintama* (after the success of a 2004 TV drama featuring the Edo-period police force). But **Sorachi** decided to feature them as side characters instead.

▶ The real-life **Shinsengumi** were a select sword-bearing brigade. They were founded in 1863 to protect the military government and run street patrols in **Kyoto**. This was at a time when Japan was beginning to open itself up to the world after a long period of isolation.

APING THE ARTIST

The creator of *Gintama* does sometimes include himself in the manga and anime. He appears in short comedy skits describing his work on the series. **Sorachi** portrays himself as a gorilla in a yellow shirt and has even worn a gorilla suit to promote *Gintama* movies.

SOCIAL SATIRE

▶ **Sorachi** makes lighthearted fun of Japanese popular culture in *Gintama*. There are jokes about **historical accuracy**, **biker gangs**, **horror tropes**, **geisha culture**, and **manga**. Sadly, many of his jokes are lost in translation, but there is plenty of slapstick and character interplay to enjoy, too.

PET PARTNER

▶ The **Yorozuya** have a notable pet that also acts as the company mascot— a huge white dog named **Sadaharu**. He was originally feted as an **Inugami** or **dog god**, one of two guardians of the Dragon Lair (the source of Altana). But, when the **Amanto** arrived, they built their space terminal over the hole and left **Sadaharu** jobless and homeless. He's lived with the **Yorozuya** ever since. Unsurprisingly for his size, **Sadaharu** has a massive appetite and leaves quite a trail behind him. He is fond of biting people's heads and should never be fed strawberry milk—it transforms him into a demon. Although he's often destructive, **Sadaharu** proves to be a savior when he prevents an invasion of giant space cockroaches. How? By lazily stomping on their queen, of course.

WHERE NEXT?

If you love *Gintama* try:

▶ **SPACE DANDY** (PICTURED)
Another sci-fi comedy that fails to follow logic, *Space Dandy* features a half-wit alien hunter crossing space with his robot assistant and a companion cat named **Me#$%***.

▶ **THE DISASTROUS LIFE OF SAIKI K.**
Student **Kusuo Saiki** is a powerful psychic who tries to keep a low profile at school. Unsurprisingly, nothing goes as planned.

▶ **SKET DANCE**
As with *Gintama's* **Yorozuya**, *SKET Dance* features a quirky trio (three high school students) offering to help with odd jobs, only to get into trouble.

TAKAHASHI RUMIKO

One of Japan's most successful and beloved manga artists, Takahashi Rumiko wowed the world, winning international acclaim for her adventure and romance titles *Urusei Yatsura*, *Maison Ikkoku*, *Ranma ½*, and *InuYasha*.

BREAKDOWN

▶ **Takahashi Rumiko** began her manga studies at the Gekiga Sonjuku school founded by **Koike Kazuo**, creator of the classic *Crying Freeman* and *Lone Wolf and Cub* (PICTURED, TOP). She followed this with two years working as an assistant for horror mangaka **Umezu Kazuo**. **Takahashi's** first professional work was the one-shot *Katte na Yatsura (Those Selfish Aliens)* that was published in 1978. The same year she began plotting her breakthrough work, the sci-fi comedy *Urusei Yatsura*. This saga ran for almost a decade and won the **Shogakukan Manga Award** in 1980.

▶ At the time, **Takahashi** was rare because she was a female creator writing for the boys' market—she picked up a great deal of female fans, too. Her next epic was aimed at slightly older readers. The romantic comedy *Maison Ikkoku* launched in 1980 and ran alongside *Urusei Yatsura* until 1987, with sporadic episodes of the titles *Mermaid Saga* and *One-pound Gospel* (a romance featuring a boxer and a nun).

▶ And the hits kept on coming . . . There was 1987's *Ranma ½* (PICTURED, BOTTOM LEFT), which is a play on martial-arts manga with a gender-bending twist, plus 1996's fantasy adventure named *InuYasha* (PICTURED, BOTTOM RIGHT) (**Shogakukan Manga Award** winner 2001) and supernatural high school drama *Rin-ne* in 2009.

▶ **Takahashi's** top-selling titles have all been adapted for anime, from *Urusei Yatsura* in 1981 to a reboot of the same title in 2022.

Lone Wolf and Cub

Ranma ½

THE CORE
KEY MANGA
Urusei Yatsura 1978–1987
Maison Ikkoku 1980–1987
Mermaid Saga 1984–1994
Ranma ½ 1987–1996
One-pound Gospel 1978–2007
Runic Theater 1987–
InuYasha 1996–2008
Rin-ne 2009–2017
Mao 2019–

KEY ANIME
Urusei Yatsura,
1981–1991, 2022–
Maison Ikkoku
1986–1988
Ranma ½ 1989–1992
InuYasha 2000–2004,
2009–2010

AWARDS
Shogakukan Manga
Award, 1980, 2001
Seiun Award, 1987, 1989
Inkpot Award, 1994
The Will Eisner Awards
Hall of Fame, 2018
Grand Prix de la ville
d'Angoulême, 2019
Japan's Medal with
Purple Ribbon, 2020
Harvey Awards Hall
of Fame, 2021

INTERNATIONAL SUPERSTAR

▶ **Takahashi's** work has been translated into many languages and has proved especially popular in English-reading markets with *Urusei Yatsura*, *Maison Ikkoku*, *Ranma ½*, *InuYasha*, and *Rin-ne* all published in the United States. She has won several international awards, including the prestigious **Will Eisner Awards Hall of Fame** (2018), **Grand Prix de la ville d'Angoulême** (2019), and **Harvey Awards Hall of Fame** (2021), while her work has influenced many Western artists including **Bryan Lee O'Malley** (Scott Pilgrim).

InuYasha

OBNOXIOUS ALIENS

▶ The fate of Planet Earth is in the hands of a hapless and lazy student! **Takahashi's** breakthrough manga, *Urusei Yatsura* (1981), begins with the threat of the alien **Oni** invading. To prevent this, the randomly chosen layabout **Moroboshu Ataru** must win a game of tag against the beautiful **Lum**, who is the daughter of the **Oni's** leader. **Ataru** wins using underhanded methods but is then misheard as proposing to **Lum**. She accepts and moves in with **Ataru** and his parents. **Ataru** then finds himself trying to fend off **Lum** and make peace with his real girlfriend, **Shinobu**.

▶ *Urusei Yatsura* (roughly translated as *Those Obnoxious Aliens*) is a sweet blend of **slapstick comedy**, **parody**, and **puns** with a huge cast of offbeat characters. Over nine years, thirty-four volumes of the manga were completed. These were adapted for four anime TV seasons and six movies. A reboot *Urusei Yatsura* TV series launched in 2022.

HOME COMFORTS

▶ While other titles by **Takahashi** may be more famous, *Maison Ikkoku* is seen as her masterwork. This is a soap opera aimed at older readers with the story set in a boarding house. It centers on **Godai Yusaku**, a hopeful college student, and **Otonashi Kyoko**, the building's manager and a recent widow.

We follow their slow progress toward finding love while dealing with peer and family expectations. Light relief is provided by a string of comic characters renting other rooms. *Maison Ikkoku* is a grown-up delight for romcom fans.

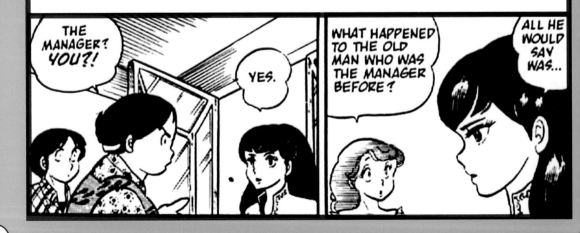

IN A SPIN

▶ *Ranma ½* puts a spin on the popular martial-arts fare after its hero, **Saotome Ranma**, and his father fall into a cursed spring. The curse means that they transform into the last creature that drowned there, if splashed with water. **Ranma** becomes a girl, and his father becomes a **panda**! The magical body-swapping makes things complicated for **Ranma** as his hand is promised to tomboy **Tendō Akane** (a daughter of the house of **Tendō Sōun**).

▶ **Ranma** gets involved in many fighting contests while avoiding a drenching and its consequences—including, fending off the attentions of rival **Kumō Tatewaki**, who is attracted to his female appearance. A dip in a magic spring leads to several other characters also becoming cartoon animals, including a pig and a duck. The comedy in the series extends to the martial-arts battles, which can involve tea ceremonies, gymnastics, and cooking!

RETURN TO THE PAST

▶ Despite massive wealth and success, **Takahashi** shows no sign of leaving the drawing board. Her current ongoing series is *Mao*—another tale that transports a modern character into ancient Japan. This time it's a girl named **Kiba Nanoka** who finds herself joining an exorcist known as **Mao** in the early 20th century. There, she helps investigate unusual supernatural deaths and unravels the mysteries of her past.

CLASSROOM OF THE ELITE

Classroom of the Elite started life as a series of light novels before also becoming manga and anime. The drama is set in a special school operated by the Japanese government for students who are the best of the best. Kōdo Ikusei Senior High School (also known as Tokyo Metropolitan Advanced Nurturing High School) has been created to monitor the students and encourage rivalry—so eventually the elite will succeed.

BREAKDOWN

▶ **Kōdo Ikusei Senior High School** is an elite school that claims to have a 100 percent employment rate for its students. It also has its own special way of teaching, and its students have way more freedom than in a normal school. For example, they can have their hair however they desire and are allowed to bring in their own personal items. When **Kijotaka** starts at the school, he is in **Class D**—the class where bad students are dumped. **Kijotaka** has a secret, though—he's super intelligent! He has his own reasons for being in **Class D**.

SNAPSHOT

▶ *Classroom of the Elite*'s creator, **Kinugasa Shōgo** is a man of mystery. He has a November birthday and supposedly lives in Fukuoka, but little else is known about him. Before creating his masterpiece, **Kinugasa** worked in game design as a writer with the artist of the light novel versions of *Classroom of the Elite*, **Tomose Shunsaku**. Since the publication of the first book in 2015, he has also worked on the manga version of the series.

THE CORE

LIGHT NOVEL
PUBLISHED BY: Media Factory
2015–2019, 2020–
WRITER: Kinugasa Shōgo
ARTIST: Tomose Shunsaku

MANGA
PRODUCED FOR: Media Factory
2016–present
WRITER: Kinugasa Shōgo
ARTIST: Ichino Yuyu
Classroom of the Elite: Horikita
2017–2018
WRITER: Kinugasa Shōgo
ARTIST: SAKAGAKI

ANIME
2017–

THE STUDENTS

The students are the stars of *Classroom of the Elite*. Although others become more prominent as the series progresses, these are the key characters at the start:

▶ **AYANOKOJI KIYOTAKA Kiyotaka** is the show's protagonist. He is a shy and retiring student with a troubled past who is also exceptionally intelligent.

▶ **HORIKITA SUZUNE Suzune** wants to be part of **Class A** and is working as hard as she can to achieve that goal.

▶ **KUSHIDA KIKYO** One of the more popular students, **Kikyo** has a friendly personality, but she also has a darker side.

▶ **HIRATA YOSUKE** The main representative of **Class D**, **Yosuke** shows signs of being an intelligent leader and seems to do things for the good of his classmates.

▶ **SUDO KEN** Perhaps the most troubled student of **Class D**, **Ken** can be something of a hothead and tends to act before thinking things through.

WHERE NEXT?

If you like *Classroom of the Elite*, try:

▶ **TORADORA! (PICTURED)**
If *Classroom of the Elite* left you a bit tense, checkout *Toradora!* This lighthearted romcom is set in a high school, and it's all about opposites attracting.

▶ **BLUE PERIOD**
Blue Period follows a high schooler who falls in love with art and decides to do all he can to get into Tokyo University of the Arts.

DEAD DEAD DEMON'S DEDEDEDE DESTRUCTION

Dead Dead Demon's Dededede Destruction is an alien invasion story with a difference—it's seen through the eyes of two teenage girls. Known as *DDDDD*, for convenience's sake, this award-winning manga has sold more than three million copies.

BREAKDOWN

▶ Three years before the start of the story, a huge spaceship appeared in the sky above Tokyo. While soldiers deal with the seemingly peaceful aliens, two high school girls—**Koyama Kadode** and **Nakagawa Ouran**—go about their daily lives but eventually learn that the real threat isn't from the aliens, but from humanity itself.

SNAPSHOT

▶ *DDDDD*'s creator is **Asano Inio**, a manga artist best known for creating character-driven stories. Before developing *DDDDD*, he created *Solanin* and *Goodnight Punpun*. He won the 2001 **GX competition** for best young manga artist and has been described as **"the voice of his generation"** by Japanese newspaper *Yomiuri Shimbun*.

THE CORE

MANGA
PUBLISHED BY: Shogakukan
2014–2022
WRITER/ARTIST: Asano Inio

ANIME
IN PRODUCTION

THE FRIENDS

▶ At the start of the series, **Koyama Kadode** and **Nakagawa Ouran** have been best friends since they were eight years old. **Kadode** is the quieter of the two, but as she grows, she starts to reveal increasing dissatisfaction with her life. **Ouran** is more flamboyant than her friend and often has crazy ideas. She's also quite a private person and only really shows her true self to her friends and family.

INVASION?

▶ The vast alien ship over Tokyo might dominate much of the story, but the nature of the aliens is only occasionally revealed—it would give too much of the story away to do so here. When they are seen, the design is wonderfully out of this world, and the manga soon asks the reader to decide what is the real danger to Tokyo—the aliens or humanity's response to them?

WHERE NEXT?

If you love *DDDDD*, try:

▶ **SHADOW STAR (NARUTARU)**
Shadow Star has the strange normality of *DDDDD*, but this time the story is about a young girl bonding with a dragonchild. It's fantasy and slice-of-life combined.

▶ **SOLANIN (PICTURED)**
Let's not forget **Asano Inio's** previous work. *Solanin* also has friendship at its core and follows two people trying to escape their humdrum lives for something better.

DORAEMON

GADGET CAT FROM THE FUTURE

Meet Japan's answer to Mickey Mouse . . . it's Doraemon!

Bright blue and packing a pouch full of impossible gadgets, this robot cat from the future is a major icon. For over 50 years, this 22nd-century catbot has been captivating fans with his mishap-filled attempts to help lazy student Nobita. Over 250 million copies of his manga adventures have been sold, and over 2,800 TV episodes and 40 animated movies have been made. *Doraemon* is the highest-grossing anime film franchise of all time. Such is his popularity, Doraemon was chosen to be Japan's anime ambassador.

BREAKDOWN

▶ Doraemon is a large blue robot cat created on September 3, 2112, by the **Matsushiba Robot Factory**. It was sent back in time by **Nobi Sewashi** to help his great-great-grandfather, 10-year-old student **Nobita**, avoid a pitiful future. **Doraemon** is able to aid **Nobita** (whose name means "falling down") with a choice of 1,293 devices kept in a four-dimensional belly pouch. Unfortunately, the use of these futuristic devices often leads to more trouble for **Nobita** and his mechanical pal.

SNAPSHOT

▶ **Fujiko F. Fujio** is the pen name of two artists, **Fujimoto Hiroshi** and **Abiko Motoo**. The duo had been collaborating since fifth grade on titles such as cute ghost adventure *Obake no Q-Tarō* and young ninja tale *Ninja Hattori-kun*.

Doraemon debuted in six educational magazines from December 1969, teaching kids from nursery school to fourth grade about body functions and the like. In 1977, he got his own title, *CoroCoro Comic*, where his cartoon adventures could run wild. After sharing an astonishing 1,345 chapters, **Fujimoto** and **Abiko** ended their partnership in 1987, and **Fujimoto** died five years later. **Abiko** passed away in 2022.

ANIME AMBASSADOR

▶ In 2008, **Doraemon** was employed as an **ambassador for anime** by **Japan's Foreign Ministry** in an official ceremony that included the presentation of the robot cat's **favorite dessert**—"dorayaki" or **red bean pancakes**.

DORAEMON DEVICES

Among the **useful items** available through **Doraemon's 4D pouch** are:

▶ Submarine
▶ Time machine
▶ Time-kerchief (a handkerchief that can change a person or object's age)
▶ Computer pencil that always writes correct exam answers
▶ Dokodemo Door (Anywhere Door that takes the pair across the universe)
▶ Translator tool
▶ Take-copter (beanie-hat bamboo-copter)
▶ Memory Bread (memory-aiding toast)
▶ Anything-Controller (a steering wheel that turns any object into a vehicle)

THE CORE

MANGA

PUBLISHED BY: Shogakukan
1,345 chapters over 45+ volumes in Japan (10 in English), 1970–1996
WRITER/ARTIST: Fujiko F. Fujio

ANIME

PRODUCED FOR: Nippon TV, 1973
Shin-Ei Animation 1978–2005
1,787 episodes
2005–
Shin-Ei Animation, 1040 episodes
42 annual animated movies

(left margin panels:)

T'S ME.

OW DID POP OUT ERE ...?

GING IN 30, RNING IN 40, S MY FATE T TERRIBLE!?

OP LYING! RE'S NO WAY CAN SEE MY FUTURE!!

42 MOVIES AND COUNTING . . .

▶ The tradition of an annual *Doraemon* movie continued in spring 2023 when Japanese fans got to see *Doraemon: Nobita's Sky Utopia*. This 42nd big-screen adventure features **Doraemon** and **Nobita** on a quest to find a perfect sky world where everyone is said to live happily. For this, they need a brand-new gadget—the **Time Zeppelin**—with its special time-warp trickery.

WHY SO BLUE?

▶ **Doraemon's** name may come from *dorayaki*, his **favorite dessert** and *mon*, Japanese for **monster** (as in *Pokémon*, *Digimon*). In the manga, however, it is claimed to come from *nora neko*, Japanese for **"stray cat."**

▶ Before jumping back in time to join **Nobita**, **Doraemon** recalls his ears were bitten off by rats when he was sleeping. He was so upset that he changed from yellow to blue—the color of sadness.

ALL GROWN UP

▶ While the manga ended in 1996, possible futures for the characters were presented in the anime movies.

In 2020, *Stand by Me Doraemon 2* saw the adult **Nobita** change his future to set up his wedding with his sweetheart, **Shizuka**.

TIME-TRAVEL TWIST

Nobi Sewashi sent Doraemon back in time to improve Nobita's life and prevent him from marrying school bully Gian (Big G)'s sister, Jaiko. Nobita is quick to reason that, if he doesn't marry Jaiko, then Sewashi won't be born as their great-great grandson. This time-travel conundrum is never explained.

FUTURE FAMILY

▶ Doraemon has a robot sister. Of course he does! Dorami, as she is known, was born on December 2, 2114, two years and two months after Doraemon. But how are they related if they were made in a factory?! Simple—they shared oil from the same can! Dorami fills in for Doraemon when he's getting his annual check-up. To avoid reminding her big brother about his lack of ears, Dorami wears a red bow on her head. She should also avoid reminding Doraemon that she's a much more advanced model than he is.

HUMAN DORAEMON

▶ The characters of Doraemon and Nobita were also licensed for advertising Toyota cars in 2011. The French movie star Jean Reno (*Godzilla, Mission: Impossible*) suited up as the robot cat in live-action clips, with the pair 20 years older than in the manga.

Dorami also starred in spin-off manga series *The Doraemons* (21 volumes from 1995–2003) and several anime (1995–2002).

TOP 10
SHŌNEN BATTLES

Shōnen manga and anime have more than their fair share of amazing battles, but the following 10 are the ones that really pack a punch. In fact, some pack punches, blasts, explosions, and high drama.

1 BLACK CLOVER

TRIAD SHOWDOWN!

▶ *Black Clover* is filled with fantastic fight scenes and deadly bad guys like Dark Triad member **Dante Zogratis**. **Asta** and his old friend **Yami** had to join forces to take down **Dante**—resulting in one of the best battles of the series. Even with the two friends fighting as one, they come close to meeting their match. While **Dante** seems unstoppable, **Asta** finally gets the win by using his **Death Thrust** spell. Explosions, magic, and swordplay not only make this a major battle but one of the key moments of the *Black Clover* saga.

FIGHTERS: Asta and Yami vs. Dant[e]

2 NARUTO SHIPPŪDEN

BRING ON THE PAIN!

▶ Let's face it, a bad guy called **Pain** sounds like he's going to be tough to beat, and their battle proves to be one of **Naruto's** best and toughest fights. **Pain** had the same teacher as **Naruto** but was corrupted by **Uchiha Obito**. His showdown with **Naruto** stretches out over several episodes with both fighters seemingly equally matched. **Pain** uses the **Animal Path** to create an animalistic attack, but **Naruto** eventually wins by pulling out his **Rasengan**—a spinning ball of chakra energy that he can use against an opponent with devastating effect.

FIGHTERS: Naruto vs. Pain

3 BLEACH

SOUL TO SOUL

▶ As a **Soul Reaper**, **Ichigo** has more than his fair share of strange and deadly confrontations. One of his toughest was against **Byakuya**. Although **Byakuya** wasn't an outright villain, he was misguided and ended up having more than one face-off against **Ichigo**. The third confrontation was the most memorable because it proved to **Byakuya** that his opponent shouldn't be underestimated. **Ichigo** also realized that taunting **Byakuya** annoyed him enough to improve his own chances. It was a tough fight that left both injured, but Ichi came out on top.

FIGHTERS: Ichi vs. Byakuya

4 DRAGONBALL Z

BLAST OFF!

▶ *Dragonball Z* was full of explosive fights, but **Goku's** confrontation with villainous **Cell** was unforgettable. **Dr. Gero** designed **Cell**, an android created using the genetics of the greatest fighters. He seemingly pummeled **Goku** during their fight, leaving the hero under a mound of rocks. **Goku** recovered and tried not to fight, but when **Cell** threatened to destroy Earth, **Goku** unleashed new levels of power. **Cell** still underestimated his opponent, and this time it proved to be a fatal mistake as **Goku** blasted **Cell** in an explosive victory.

FIGHTERS: Goku vs. Cell

5 ONE PIECE
KICK OFF!

▶ **Doflamingo** was a powerful pirate captain and king of the **Dressrosa** before facing off against **Luffy**. It wasn't their first meeting—**Luffy** had already punched the pirate captain, but their final bout was by far their toughest. It came just in time for pirate **Trafalgar Law**, who **Doflamingo** was about to kill by stomping on his head. **Luffy's** foot saved the day, blocking the pirate's attack. The ensuing fight between them was tough on both and saw **Luffy** use **Gear 4** for the first time to eventually defeat his enemy.

6 HUNTER x HUNTER
SHOWDOWN!

▶ With the heroes using their life force to enhance their own fighting styles, *Hunter x Hunter* has more than its fair share of epic battles. One of the best is also one of the most shocking when **Netero** takes on **Meruem**, the strongest of the **Chimera Ants**. **Meruem** planned to take over the world but allow humanity to live on—under his control. He can kill with just a lightning flick of his tail, but **Netero** was a seasoned warrior. To say it was a close fight would be an understatement, with **Netero** only winning in the end by sacrificing his own life to defeat **Meruem**.

FIGHTERS: Netero vs. Meruem

7 MY HERO ACADEMIA
HEROIC ATTACK!

▶ Some of the best fights in anime and manga are not good versus evil, but hero fighting hero. That's the case with this classic clash between **Midoriya** and **Todoroki** in *My Hero Academia*. The confrontation had been building for a while, and soon both heroes were unleashing their full power at each other—**Midoriya's One For All** ability is countered by **Todoroki's Quirk**: Half-Cold Half-Hot, which uses fire and ice. Not only was it a ferocious fight, but it also revealed new aspects of both heroes, leaving them with a new understanding of their abilities and each other.

FIGHTERS: Midoriya vs. Todoroki

8 BAKI THE GRAPPLER

UNCHAINED AND UNLEASHED!

▶ With a show and manga called *Baki the Grappler*, it's no surprise there are some exceptional fights—after all, the story is about **Baki** trying to be the best fighter he can by taking on dangerous opponents. One of his toughest contests takes place when he infiltrates a jail just to take on **Biscuit Oliva** (aka **Mr. Unchained**). **Biscuit** is a superstrong assassin working as a prison guard. **Baki** wins, and then **Unchained** makes sure **Baki** gets out of jail to get to his next fight.

FIGHTERS: Baki vs. Mr. Unchained

9 DEMON SLAYER THE MOVIE: MUGEN TRAIN

DIE HARD!

▶ A direct follow-up to the *Demon Slayer* series, *Mugen Train* is filled with tense battles. One of the deadliest takes place between the heroic **Rengoku** and the demon **Akaza**. The two clash in a storm of magical energy and **Akaza**—impressed with his opponent's skills —tries persuading him to become a demon. **Rengoku** refuses and **Akaza**, after a ferocious confrontation, finally lands a killing blow. Despite the fatal attack, **Rengoku** still refuses to become a demon and tries to behead **Akaza** as he nears his own demise.

FIGHTERS: Rengoku vs. Akaza

10 MADE IN ABYSS: DAWN OF THE DEEP SOUL

DEEP DIVE!

▶ Sometimes anime action can take you by surprise. The excellent *Made in Abyss* isn't well known for fight scenes, but *Made in Abyss: Dawn of the Deep Soul* features one of the best as the main heroes come face to face with **Bondrewd**. Also known as the **"Lord of the Dawn,"** **Bondrewd** is a **Delver** who doesn't let morality get in the way of his research. With **Riko** and **Nanachi** planning their attack carefully while **Reg** attacks directly, it's a tense fight. With a villain as hard to kill as **Bondrewd**, victory doesn't always mean the end of the war.

FIGHTERS: Bondrewd vs. Riko, Reg, and Nanachi

HOW TO DRAW . . .

VILLAINS

Let your evil side loose with this step-by-step
lesson in drawing a master villain.

STEP 1

Begin by lightly drawing a stick
figure holding an imperious
pose. Mark his head and joints
with circles.

STEP 2

Now, block in his body.
The legs are placed tightly
together here, and his hair
is taller than his head.

STEP 3

STEP 4

Add the wide shoulders and flowing folds of the villain's coat. Sketch his fingers and smoke rising from one raised hand.

Finally, draw a ghoulish grinning face, spiky hair, and the folds and details in his freaky costume.

FEMALE MONSTER

Villains come in all shapes and sizes. Here's a fantasy female monster with the feathery top half of a bird of prey and the tail of a sea serpent.

MUSCULAR THUG

Beef up a baddy with some oversized muscles. Give him a neck wider than his head and a super-tight T-shirt to show off his pecs.

WARLORD

A fantasy demon lord needs a skull-like face, horned helmet, over-the-top armor, and a cape he could trip over.

DARK MASTER NINJA

While he can strike a pose to match a ninja hero, this guy shows he's nasty with his bushy eyebrows, tiny eyes, and mean-looking facial hair.

SHINKAI MAKOTO

Shinkai Makoto has been hailed by many critics as the new Miyazaki.

He is one the most successful and exciting writers and directors to come out of Japan in the last two decades—especially after his masterpiece *Your Name.* outperformed **Miyazaki's** classic *Spirited Away* at the box office.

THE EARLY DAYS

▶ Born on February 9, 1973, **Shinkai Makoto** studied Japanese literature at Chuo University and graduated in 1996. After college he started working on video clips for games at **Falcom**. It was during this time that he met musician **Tenmon**, who would later provide the soundtracks for many of his early films. While working at **Falcom**, **Shinkai** also created a short five-minute animation called *She and Her Cat*. The film was shot from the cat's viewpoint and won several awards. While producing another short, *Voices of a Distant Star*, he left **Falcom** so that he could work full-time on the animation. His first full feature was *The Place Promised in Our Early Days* in 2004. The film was set in an alternate Japan, half of which had been occupied by the Soviet Union following the end of World War II. It was a box office smash.

BECOMING A MASTER

▶ In 2007 **Shinkai** released the anthology movie called *5 Centimeters per Second*. This was followed in 2011 by *Children Who Chase Lost Voices*—a coming-of-age story involving lost love and magic. *The Garden of Words* (PICTURED) was released in 2013, which was a slice-of-life fable about the friendship between a 15-year-old boy and a 27-year-old woman. Both films were critically acclaimed, but it was his next work that would bring the creator worldwide fame—the modern-day classic *Your Name*.

RECENT WORK

▶ **Shinkai** followed *Your Name.* with *Weathering with You* in 2019. This romantic fantasy is about a young boy who runs away and meets a girl who can control the weather. It was another award-winning success, cementing **Shinkai's** reputation as a modern-day great in the world of film and anime. It was followed by *Suzume* in 2022, which was about a high school girl and a strange young man who travel throughout Japan trying to prevent disasters.

FAMILY TIES

▶ **Shinkai** is married to **Misaka Chieko**, a retired actress and producer. The couple's daughter, **Niitsu Chise** was born in 2010 and now works as a child actor.

WHO KNEW

Shinkai's favorite films include *Laputa: Castle in the Sky*, *Nausicaä of the Valley of the Wind*, *The Castle of Cagliostro*, and *The End of Evangelion*.

KEY ANIME

The Place Promised in Our Early Days 2004
5 Centimeters per Second 2007
Children Who Chase Lost Voices 2011
The Garden of Words 2013
Your Name. 2016
Weathering with You 2019
Suzume 2022

CHIHAYAFURU

Chihayafuru is a josei manga about a young girl's love of karuta—a card game that's popular in Japan and is linked to literature. This manga has sold over 28 million copies and has won countless awards—it's even been credited with a rise in popularity for karuta. The series blends sports manga with romance and drama. It's not only been turned into a successful anime, but three live-action movies, too. The series is often hailed as one of the best anime of the 2010s.

BREAKDOWN

▶ **Ayase Chihaya** has spent most of her young life supporting her sister's modeling career. When she meets fellow student **Wataya Arata**, however, she discovers a love for **karuta** and seems to have a natural gift for the card game. She realizes that if she became the number one **karuta** player in Japan, it would make her number one in the world. She joins the **Mizusawa Karuta Club**, and as she starts her rise to the top of the **karuta** game, she also tries to come to terms with her feelings for her friends.

SNAPSHOT

▶ *Chihayafuru*'s creator **Suetsugu Yuki** published her first work, *Taiyō no Romance*, in *Nakayoshi* magazine in 1992. Her other early work included *Kimi no Shiroi Hane* and *Flower of Eden*—both published in the popular shōjo manga magazine *Bessatsu Friend*. *Chihayafuru* started in 2007 and went on to win several awards including a **Manga Taisho Award** (2009) and a **Kodansha Manga Award** in the shōjo category (2011).

THE CORE

MANGA
PUBLISHED BY: Kodansha
50 volumes, 2007–2022
WRITER/ARTIST: Suetsugu Yuki

ANIME
2011–2020
74 episodes and OVAs

MOVIES
Chihayafuru: Kami no Ku 2016
Chihayafuru: Shimo no Ku 2016
Chihayafuru: Musubi 2018

JOSEI MANGA

▶ **Josei manga** translates as **"women's comics."** The genre started to develop its own identity in the 1980s. There's also **shōjo manga**, which is a style aimed at teenage girls and young women—though in recent times, both **shōjo** and **josei** have blended into each other.

WHAT'S IN A NAME?

▶ The manga's title *Chihayafuru* means **"tremendous power."** It is also linked to a poem by one of Japan's greatest poets, **Ariwara no Narihira**.

WHAT IS KARUTA?

▶ Japan's popular card game **karuta** dates back to the 19th century and is especially popular with girls. It is usually made up of two sets of cards—one with images and one with words. Competition cards contain famous poems. A reader starts reading a poem or proverb, and the players must find the image card that matches it before their opponent. The best players are those who memorize the 100 classic poems so they can react faster than their opponents when the reader starts.

PLAYING TO WIN

▶ **Karuta** rules were unified by the **Tokyo Karuta Association** for the first competitive tournament held in 1904. Attempts were made to set up a national association in 1934. This finally resulted in the **All Japan Karuta Association** in 1957. The winner of the male game gains the title **Meijin**, with the female game winner named the **Queen**—both are also known as **Grand Champions**. If someone wins seven times, they are named an **Eternal Champion**. The first international tournament took place in 2012, and by 2018, it featured players from eight nations.

THE PLAYERS

▶ AYASE CHIHAYA

Chihaya was inspired to play **karuta** by **Arata** while she was in elementary school and was soon dreaming of becoming Japan's greatest player. She is obsessed with the game—so much so that her friends call her "karuta baka" (karuta crazy). She has feelings for both **Arata** and **Taichi**.

▶ WATAYA ARATA

Arata is the grandson of a master **karuta** player. He transferred to **Chihaya's** school when he was young and inspired her to take up the game. He's very quiet and kind, and loves **karuta**. He has an exceptional memory, which really helps his game play.

▶ MASHIMA TAICHI

Chihaya's best friend is **Taichi**, a confident, good-looking student who excels in both his studies and sports. His mother pressured him into entering competitions that he was sure he'd win.

LIVE ACTION

▶ The manga and anime's success led to a trilogy of live-action movies. The first, *Chihayafuru: Kami no Ku*, was released in 2016 and starred **Hirose Suzu** as **Chihaya**. The second, *Chihayafuru: Shimo no Ku*, followed in 2016, with the final part of the trilogy, *Chihayafuru: Musubi*, released two years later. There was also a live-action spin-off series on Hulu Japan.

JUNIOR FLASHBACK

▶ The success of the main manga led to a spin-off with a four-book light novel series following the main characters through their junior high school years. It was adapted into manga by **Tōda Oto** and it ran from October 2017 to December 2018. There was also a special fan book published in 2012, containing facts about the characters as well as experts providing tips on how to play **karuta**.

WHERE NEXT?

If you enjoyed *Chihayafuru*, try:

▶ **KONO OTO TOMARE!** (PICTURED)
When **Takezou** ends up as the only member of his school's club for **koto** players (**koto** is a traditional Japanese string instrument), he soon has to deal with an influx of new members.

▶ **SHAKUNETSU NO TAKKYUU MUSUME**
Set in the world of junior high school **Ping-Pong**, the story follows new student **Koyori** as she joins the team and tries to win back the school's recently lost champion status.

▶ **OFFSIDE**
This sports manga deals with **soccer** and follows **goalkeeper Goro Kumagaya**. He hoped to join the school that had the best soccer team, but it doesn't work out. Instead he finds himself on a team struggling to be the best they can. Things look up when **Goro** realizes that he's a far better striker than **goalkeeper**.

THE PROMISED NEVERLAND

Mixing classic manga storytelling with echoes of *Peter Pan*, *The Promised Neverland* is a scary all-ages thrill ride. Starting in a mysterious orphanage, the young heroes soon find that their home isn't as nice as it seems. And when their friends leave, they're not getting adopted but instead being fed to demons. With such a stunning premise, its hardly surprising *The Promised Neverland* has won countless awards and become one of the best-selling manga of all time.

BREAKDOWN

▶ Set in 2045, *The Promised Neverland* takes place one thousand years after **The Promise**— a treaty between humans and demons that let both live in their own worlds, but it also allowed demons to create special breeding farms of humans for their own consumption. Some of these are known as orphanages to the unsuspecting children growing up there. When two children, **Emma** and **Norman**, follow their friend, **Conny**, as she is taken for "adoption," they learn the truth. When **Norman** is also taken, **Emma** and her friend **Ray** not only try to escape but also find a way to save all their friends.

SNAPSHOT

▶ Writer **Shirai Kaiu** delivered a 300-page proposal for *The Promised Neverland* to *Weekly Shōnen Jump* editor **Sugita Suguru**. After a wide search for artists, they chose D**emizu Posuka** as the illustrator. While **Shirai** had been producing published work since 2015's *The Location of Ashley-Gate* for *Shōnen Jump+*, **Demizu** had been working as a manga and anime artist since 2008—starting with a miniseries for *CoroCoro magazine*. She enjoyed employing different art styles on *The Promised Neverland* to contrast the brightness of the children with the darkness of the demons.

THE CORE

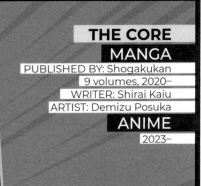

MANGA
PUBLISHED BY: Shogakukan
9 volumes, 2020–
WRITER: Shirai Kaiu
ARTIST: Demizu Posuka

ANIME
2023–

NIGHTMARISH INSPIRATION

▶ **Shirai Kaiu** has said that the idea for the story was partly inspired by his own childhood nightmares of demons eating children—possibly the result of his love of **Western fairy tales** such as *Hansel and Gretel*, as well as Japanese mythology. **"All these fears, ideas, influences, have come together. This is how the story of *The Promised Neverland* was born,"** the writer claimed in an interview.

THE ORPHANAGE

▶ **Emma** and her friends have been raised in the **Grace Field House** orphanage. They're happy there, watched over by "Mom." They all have a warm bed, delicious food, all-white uniforms, and an ID number on their necks. The children want for nothing but are warned not to venture beyond the orphanage grounds. There are several orphanages in the **demon realm**, each used as breeding grounds for the demons' food supply.

WHERE NEXT?

If you love *The Promised Neverland*, try:

▶ **BUNGO STRAY DOGS** (PICTURED)
Like the heroes of *The Promised Neverland*, some of those in *Bungo Stray Dogs* are orphans with special gifts. Unlike their counterparts, they're not on the run from demons but out trying to capture criminals and solve crimes.

ANIME SPORTS MOVES

Sports anime and manga are hugely popular. Check out page 20 for some of the best. Within sports manga many players have a super-move they use to win a game. Sometimes these can be realistic, other times they're out of this world!

1 EYESHIELD 21

DEVIL BAT GHOST

PLAYER: Sena

▶ **Sena** has been bullied and chased all his life. It's one of the things that makes him fast and hard to catch—perfect qualities for **American football**. He is given the name **Eyeshield 21** to protect his identity from other teams who might try to snatch him. **Sena's** ability to run and not get caught soon becomes legendary, especially when he uses his **Devil Bat Ghost** move, which seems to make him disappear only to reappear farther up the field. With a skill like that, there's only one thing left to say: **"Touchdown!"**

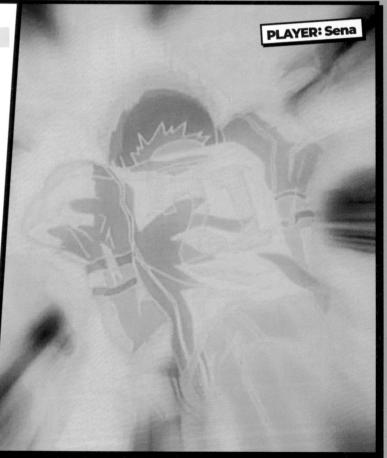

2 EYESHIELD 21

MAGIC ARMS

PLAYER: Habashira Rui

▶ Speaking of **American football**, it's not just **Sena's** team that has the skills. While **Sena** faced plenty of opponents with strange skills, one of the hardest players to beat was **Habashira Rui** of the **Zokugaku Champions**. **Rui's** arms were exceptionally long and could snap out at lightning speed. His snakelike tongue was a family trait, but he also had astonishing speed—perfect for grabbing players as they tried to pass him or for intercepting a pass in midair. It's why he was one of the best linebackers in the game.

PLAYER: Habashira Rui

3 KUROKO'S BASKETBALL

HIGH PROJECTILE THREE

▶ **Basketball** is a fast-moving game, and the best players not only need lightning-fast reflexes but lightning-fast minds, too. **Midorima Shintarō** has both. His specialist shot is the **High Projectile Three**. He can throw the ball into the basket from anywhere on the court, thanks to his pinpoint accuracy and ability to calculate trajectories. The skill also gives him self-doubt, though, and if there's a chance he could miss, he often fails to take a shot altogether.

YER: Midorima

4 THE PRINCE OF TENNIS

PINNACLE OF PERFECTION

▶ **Echizen Ryoma** is a **tennis** prodigy. *The Prince of Tennis* follows his rise through the sport and eventual mastery of the **Pinnacle of Perfection**. Rather than a single move, this is a state of mind achieved from complex training routines. It enables players to take techniques they have seen others perform and use them to go beyond their own natural abilities. It's a state of mind that enables true champions to be victorious, as **Echizen Ryoma** proves!

PLAYER: Echizen Ryoma

5 KUROKO'S BASKETBALL

VISUAL COMPREHENSION SKILL

▶ It's back to high school **basketball** for the next entry and **Ryōta Kise's** ability to copy any move he sees on court. Although a superb athlete (not to mention good-looking and tall), it's his visual comprehension skill that helped make him an MVP. He can duplicate any moves he's seen and mix them together to create new moves that are truly game-changing. Talk about a slam dunk!

PLAYER: Ryōta Kise

6 KUROKO'S BASKETBALL

EMPEROR EYE

▶ **Basketball** is about speed, skill, and tactics. It also helps if you can spot an opponent's weak points—something **Akashi Seijūrō** does all too well when he uses the **Emperor Eye** technique. This skill allows a player to see another player's body in great detail, such as their breathing and muscle weaknesses. Not only that, but he can use this skill on his teammates to see how they're faring in a game and which ones have the greatest potential. It even helps him copy another's moves by watching them closely. Needless to say, it's a game-changing skill!

PLAYER: Akashi Seijūrō

7 HAJIME NO IPPO

THE DEMPSEY ROLL

▶ **Boxing's** a tough sport and *Hajime no Ippo (The First Step)* is a brutal **boxing** tale following a young fighter's rise. The hero, **Makunouchi Ippo**, is a boxer who has mastered the famous **"Dempsey Roll,"** which is a real-life move named after the legendary boxer **Jack Dempsey**. The move needs to be seen to be believed and involves the **boxer** launching a flurry of blows at his opponent. **Ippo** refines the famous technique to get the most out of it and become a champion. You could say it's a real knockout . . .

PLAYER: Makunouchi Ippo

8 INAZUMA ELEVEN

THE GOD HAND

▶ Lots of players in *Inazuma Eleven* have special powers, but one of the best belongs to goalkeeper **Mark Evans**, who has a **God Hand** ability. Anyone who's ever played in goal would want this skill—**Mark** can create a hand out of lightning that can catch any non-superpowered shot. **Mark** inherited the power from his grandfather, and it proved to be a real shot-stopper!

PLAYER: Mark Evans

9 YOWAMUSHI PEDAL GO!

HIGH CADENCE CLIMB TECHNIQUE

▶ **Cycling** is fun, but it's also a super tough sport. In *Yowamushi Pedal Go!* **Onoda Sakamichi** finds his true calling as part of a cycling team and works his way up to become **captain of the Sohoku High Bicycle Racing Club** and its best member.
He finds riding with the team improves his performance—especially when he uses his **High Cadence Climb technique** to zoom up hilly courses.

PLAYER: Onoda Sakamichi

10 LITTLE WITCH ACADEMIA

GHOST HUNTING

▶ Okay, so it's not a real-life sport, but it should be. In *Little Witch Academia* the annual sport is **ghost hunting**. It takes place annually over 12 days, with **Wild Hunters** donning special gear and riding wolves in the sky as they hunt. They also carry magical weaponry to help them banish their ghostly prey. It can be a highly dangerous sport, and in one early hunt a ghost of a bear called **Devil Claw** went berserk and killed several hunters. Luckily for us mortals, ghosts can only be seen by those with magical abilities.

PLAYER: Everyone involved

MANGA AND ANIME:
TIMELINE

Manga and anime have a long and impressive history. Here are some of the mediums' key moments, best-loved stories, and major milestones.

1902 THE BEGINNING

▶ *Jiji Manga*—supplement in the Sunday edition of the leading newspaper *Jiji Shinpo (Current Events)* debuts as cartoonist **Kitazawa Rakuten** becomes first person to use the word **manga** in its modern usage. **Kitazawa** is thought of as the "father of manga."

1907 *SHŌNEN PUCK*

▶ *Shōnen Puck* is the first manga magazine published for children.

1934 I ROBOT TANK!

▶ *Tank Tankuro* by **Sakamoto Gajo** is published. Widely regarded as the first robot-like character in manga, the hero had a round robot-like body that could produce anything he wanted from a hole in his belly.

1950 THE WHITE LION
▶ *Jungle Tatei (Kimba the White Lion)* starts in *Manga Shōnen*.

1945 FIRST ANIME
▶ Japan's first homegrown anime, *Momotaro's Divine Sea Warriors*, directed by **Seo Mitsuyo**, hits screens.

1947 SHŌNEN
Manga Shōnen, a new manga magazine starts.

1952 ASTRO BOY FLIES!
▶ *Astro Boy* starts in *Shōnen* magazine and would prove to be one of the most influential manga of all time. The original Japanese title translates as *The Mighty Atom*.

1952 PRINCESS KNIGHT
▶ *Princess Knight* starts in *Shōjo Club*; although not the first manga aimed at young girls, it quickly becomes one of the most popular.

1947 NEW FORMAT
▶ *Shin-Takarajima (New Treasure Island)* (1946) by **Shichima Sakai** and **Tezuka Osamu** is published. It's a bestseller—first in the tankōbon format (a one-off book that's not part of a series).

1948 STUDIO TIME
▶ The first anime studio is formed, **Nihon Dogo Co.**, which eventually evolved into **Toei Animation**.

1961 ANIME TV SERIES!
▶ The first anime TV series, *Otogi Manga Calendar*, starts on May 1.

1957 ENTER THE NINJA
▶ *Ninja Bugeichō (Ninja Martial Arts Handbook)* by **Sanpei Shirato** begins—one of the first popular manga aimed at an older male audience.

1954 SHŌJO TIME
▶ *Nakayoshi*, a shōjo (girls) manga launches. It would become one of the best-selling manga of that style.

1959 SHŌNEN IN ACTION
▶ *Shōnen Book Monthly* begins, the predecessor to *Weekly Shōnen Jump* magazine.

1956 GIANT ROBOTS AHOY!
▶ *Tetsujin 28* by **Yokoyama Mitsuteri** starts. The first story of a giant robot controlled by someone with a remote control. It's often regarded as the first mecha story.

1956 WEEKLY MANGA
▶ *Weekly Manga Times* launches, the first manga weekly.

1958 THE WHITE SERPENT
▶ *Tale of the White Serpent*, the first anime movie, is released, created by **Toei Animation** studios.

1958 MOLE'S ADVENTURE
▶ First full-color animation, *Mogura no Adventure (Mole's Adventure)* airs on Japan TV on July 14.

1966 *BATMAN!*

▶ Manga *Batman* strips appear in *Shōnen King* magazine.

1966 COLOR TV

▶ *Jungle Tatei (Kimba the White Lion)* by **Tezuka Osamu** is the first color anime TV series.

1966 *SHŌNEN* RULES!

▶ *Shōnen* sales hit 1 million.

1966 *SALLY THE WITCH*

▶ *Sally the Witch* is released—the first anime aimed at girls.

1963 *ASTRO BOY* HITS TV!

▶ January 1. *Astro Boy* starts on New Year's Day—the first really popular anime.

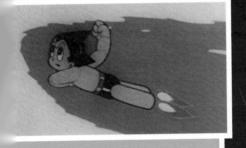

1964 CYBORGS!

▶ *Cyborg 009*, a long-running popular manga, starts in *Weekly Shōnen King*.

1967 ACTION ASSASSIN!

▶ *Manga Action*, a new manga title, begins.

1967 *LUPIN III*

▶ *Lupin III*, an action comedy manga about an assassin, starts in *Weekly Manga Action*.

1968 WEEKLY SHŌNEN

▶ The greatest magazine of all—*Weekly Shōnen Jump!*—begins. It would go on to be one of the most popular manga anthologies, selling over 7.5 billion copies.

1968 *TOMORROW'S JOE*

▶ *Tomorrow's Joe* begins in *Weekly Shōnen Manga*, becoming a popular boxing manga. It was adapted into a popular anime in 1970. When one of the characters died in 1970, the publisher held a funeral for them.

1970 LONE WOLF

▶ *Lone Wolf and Cub* starts in *Weekly Manga Action*. Written by **Koike Kazuo** and illustrated by **Kojima Goseki**, the violent story of a Rōnin (rogue samurai) and small child was hugely popular. It not only became a TV series and multiple movies but also heavily influenced US comics such as *Daredevil* and TV shows like *The Mandalorian*.

1969 ROBOTIC CAT!

▶ *Doraemon* begins. Originally published in *CoroCoro Comic*, the strip—a comedy about a robotic cat that travels back from the 22nd century to help a lazy kid—went on to become a huge hit.

1969 *GOLGO 13*

▶ *Golgo 13*—an action manga about an assassin—starts in *Big Comic*. It would go on to be the world's longest-running manga.

1973 MAKING HISTORY

▶ *Barefoot Gen* starts—a series based on personal accounts of surviving the bombing of Hiroshima.

1974 ALPINE HEROIN[E]

▶ *Heidi, Girl of the Alps* anime is broadcast in Jap[an]. It becomes one of the firs[t] anime to gain an international release.

1975 CANDY CLUB

▶ *Candy Candy* by **Mizuki Kyōko** in *Nakayoshi* starts. It was not only popular but also went on to win the first **Kodansha Manga Award** for Shōjo in 1977.

1979 *YOUNG JUMP* MAGAZINE

▶ *Young Jump* magazine starts. It is a companion mag to *Weekly Shōnen Jump* aimed at young men.

1981 LOVING THE ALIEN

▶ *Urusei Yatsura* begins. The popular comedy about an alien who believes she's married to a human went on to be one of the best-selling manga of all time.

1981 *CAPTAIN TSUBASA*

▶ *Captain Tsubasa* begins. Written by **Takahashi Yōichi**, this long-running manga about a young soccer player would go on to be a popular anime series.

1979 THIS MEANS WAR!

▶ *Mobile Suit Gundam* airs for the first time. It would spawn a hugely successful toy line and is one of the shows responsible for the rise of giant robots in manga and anime.

1982 KEY MANGA

▶ *Akira* begins in *Young Magazine*. *Akira* would become one of the most influential manga and anime ever.

1983 *POSTAPOCALYPTIC STORY*

▶ *Fist of the North Star* starts in *Weekly Shōnen Jump*. This violent postapocalyptic story would go on to be a successful anime.

1985 PSYCHIC!

▶ *Mai the Psychic Girl* becomes one of the first manga to be released in Japanese and English at the same time.

1985 CRYING FREEMAN

▶ This famous and violent manga about an assassin who sheds tears for his victims launches in *Big Comics Spirits*.

1984 POWER BALL!

▶ *Dragon Ball* begins in *Weekly Shōnen Jump*. It would go on to be a hugely successful franchise.

1984 POWER OF THE WIND

▶ *Nausicaä of the Valley of the Wind* is released to critical acclaim.

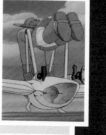

1988 WORLDWIDE SUCCESS!

▶ *Akira* is released as an anime. It becomes hugely successful and helps bring anime and manga to the whole world.

1989 SIGNED AND DELIVERED!

▶ *Kiki's Delivery Service* becomes the highest-earning movie of the year in Japan.

1989 *BATTLE ANGEL ALITA*

▶ *Gunnmu* starts in *Business Jump*. It would become better known by its Western name *Battle Angel Alita*.

1992 BESTSELLER FOR GIRLS!

▶ *Sailor Moon* begins in *Nakayoshi* magazine and would become one of the most popular girls manga of all time.

1993 MANGA MANIA!

▶ *Manga Mania is* released in the UK—the country's first Manga monthly.

1991 UK ANIME!

▶ *Anime UK* starts, giving the UK its first regular anime magazine.

1991 *GHOST IN THE SHELL*

▶ *Ghost in the Shell* by **Shirow Masmune** begins in *Young Magazine*. It would go on to become a successful anime and Hollywood blockbuster.

1994 CASE CLOSED!

▶ *Detective Conan* starts in *Weekly Shōnen Jump*. Due to legal problems with the name, it was translated into English as *Case Closed*.

INFO ON THOSE GUYS!!

THEY MIGHT HAVE...

1995 *EVANGELION!*

▶ *Neon Genesis Evangelion* (often known as simply *Evangelion on Evi*) airs for the first time and would become one of the most successful animes of the decade.

1996 COLLECT THEM ALL!

▶ *Yu-Gi-Oh!* begins in *Weekly Shōnen Jump* and would go on to create a huge franchise of anime, manga, and cards.

1996 CATCH THEM ALL!

▶ *Pokémon* is launched and would go on to be one of the most successful franchises ever. What started as a **Nintendo** game soon launched as cards, manga, and anime.

1996 *PRINCESS MONONOKE*

▶ *Princess Mononoke* is released. Critically acclaimed, the film would also become the first anime to win an award for best picture at the 21st Japan Academy Awards.

1997 THE FORCE IS MANGA!

▶ *Star Wars* by **Tamaki Hisao** is published in Japan. The English-language version published by **Dark Horse** would win an Eisner Award in 1999.

2001 AWARD WINNER!
▶ *Spirited Away* is released in Japan. It would go on to win several awards including a 2003 Academy Award for Best Animated Feature.

2001 *BLEACH*
▶ *Bleach* by **Kubo Tite** starts in *Weekly Shōnen Jump.*

2006 THE NOTEBOOK
▶ *Death Note* begins in *Weekly Shōnen Jump.*

2009 INVASION!
▶ *Attack on Titan* launches in *Bessatsu Shōnen Magazine.*

2003 SHŌNEN USA!
▶ *Shōnen Jump,* a US monthly magazine, begins.

2003 NEW *ASTRO BOY*
▶ *Astro Boy* returns as a new anime.

2020 DEMON TRAIN
▶ *Demon Slayer: Mugen Train* makes over $400 million at the Japanese box office.

PICTURE CREDITS

(A) = Anime (M) = Manga